FAUX CHIC

QUARRY

FAUX CHIC

CAROL ENDLER STERBENZ & GENEVIEVE A. STERBENZ

QUARRY BOOKS

First published in the United States of America by
Quarry Books, an imprint of
Rockport Publishers, Inc.
33 Commercial Street
Gloucester, Massachusetts 01930-5089
Telephone: (978) 282-9590
Fax: (978) 283-2742
www.rockpub.com

Library of Congress Cataloging-in-Publication data available

ISBN 1-59253-115-6

10 9 8 7 6 5 4 3 2 1

Design: Yee Design
Cover Image: Brian Harrison/Red Cover
Back Cover Image: Courtesy of Laura Ashley, Ltd.
Project Manager/Copy Editor: Stacey Ann Follin
Proofreader: Karen Diamond

Printed in China

WARNING: Always make certain that your workplace is safe and your tools and materials are in the
proper condition. You should be sure to follow the manufacturer's operating instructions, obey all
local laws and codes, take safety precautions, and use your best judgment. All do-it-yourself projects
involve some risk, and the publisher, editors, and authors take no responsibility for any injury or loss
arising from the procedures or materials described in this book. Materials, tools, skills, and work
areas vary greatly and are the responsibility of the reader. The directions for projects in this book
are for guidance only. Individual results will vary.

Dedication

For my sister, Anne

C.E.S.

For Rodney,

My younger brother and my oldest friend.

G.A.S.

Contents

THE FAUX CHIC HOME

The Bedroom **90**

The Bathroom **114**

Introduction

FOR THE FIRST TIME, IN ONE VOLUPTUOUS COMPENDIUM ENTITLED *FAUX CHIC*, you have at your fingertips all the inspiration and direction you need to transform your rooms into living spaces that are quintessentially chic. Interpreting the hallmarks of chic style—color, luxury, elegance, and comfort, together with intrinsic individuality, resourcefulness, and practicality—*Faux Chic* focuses on both formal and informal schemes for every room of the house. It shows you how to incorporate faux finishes and effects (provided by paints, paper, carvings, trims, tassels, and the like) so that all the architectural details, furniture, and fabrics in your home convey the aesthetic coherency and, above all, the indomitable spirit of chic style.

Although the French word *faux* means "false," it is important to state at the outset that creating a faux chic interior does not mean that the spaces in your home will be fake—quite the contrary. Instead, faux chic is a decorating philosophy that encourages you to express your unique creativity and imagination in all your surroundings, using faux effects that allow you to fill your interiors with the furniture and objects *you* have chosen or approved. You can mix and match the new and the old, the delicate and the sturdy—ultimately, making accessible decorations that might otherwise be out of reach because of their rarity and high cost. With faux chic, you can impart your stylistic inclinations to your home, whether you want one inspired by, say, a Parisian flat, a Tuscan villa, an English cottage, a New York loft, or an amiable combination of them all. The most important underpinnings of faux chic are that your home be authentic to you and that you articulate all its workings into an evolving archive of your life, one that transcends a particular trend and period style, one that satisfies your chic self.

Faux Chic provides not only a philosophy but also a practical approach to using faux techniques to help you achieve a chic style that reflects the truth about what you value and what you love. It shows you how you can manipulate color, texture, pattern, or any other design element, to patinate, age, texturize, and color walls, floors, and furniture. You will see how to reproduce the wear-and-tear effects and surface finishes that might ordinarily take centuries to achieve. By applying the faux effects to simulate aging paint, for example, you can transform an ordinary pine table into a valuable reproduction that looks like you lifted it out of a previous century.

Faux Chic is about more than making convincing copies, however. It is also about adding originality to your designs by applying special painterly effects and surface embellishments. Suddenly, moldings and carvings can add drama and depth to a flat wall. A sequence of tinted glazes manipulated with a rag can reproduce the texture and beauty of a wall in a period interior.

But Faux Chic is not just devoted to the large-scale statements that any home interior makes. It also features the more subtle decorations that reveal in intimate detail the character and experience of the people who inhabit the space, from a haphazard collection of mismatched china plates that are displayed on a mantel and surrounded by bouquets of dried and fresh flowers to a stack of vintage suitcases that serves as a side table—plates found for a few dollars at a flea market, bouquets preserved from occasions past, and valises pulled out of the attic. Ultimately, with the faux chic approach, you will be able to create interiors that are harmoniously chic in style and infused with idiosyncratic touches that only you can add.

Central to achieving a faux chic interior is a constellation of design elements, each of which is easy to identify and to exploit according to your unique preferences. One element is color. Whether expressed in faded, subtle hues or in soothing or jarring tones, or used singularly or in combination with others, color can be used on everything from your walls and floors, to your furniture and soft furnishings, down to the smallest decorative detail. Whether you choose to cover your walls in a raspberry and cream textile or place one red velvet pillow on a white chair, color creates impact. It is one of the most powerful communicators of the felt sense of an interior. It can also communicate place. You can choose between Marie Antoinette's blue and the ultramarine of the Mediterranean, or between a madder red from the Middle East and a grayed-out red from American colonial times. Faux Chic is eclectic in its approach to color, inspiring you to mix and match color as well as pattern and texture in a way congruous with your styling decisions. Although admittedly subjective in character, attractive colorways are suggested through the exquisite photographs that show entire room settings as well as detailed vignettes. You are encouraged to experiment with color combinations using the illustrations as inspiration.

Faux Chic is also about timeless elegance and luxury, and its pages reveal furniture and decorations that cover a wide range of periods and styles—from a carved Louis XV chair, reflecting the aristocratic silhouettes of past centuries, to an Eames chair made of polystyrene, pointing to the more fluid forms of contemporary time. A chic interior contains a mix of materials from hardwoods to soft textiles. It gathers well-worn pillows, made in the most luxurious brocades and velvets, and places them on an aged wooden bench with chipped, peeling paint. It pairs embroidered linen with animal-print throws and anything that shows its pedigree, even if a bit tattered, grimy, or chipped. Faux Chic shows that good quality and good taste never go out of fashion, and that the evidence of aging and wear does not detract from the value of a piece, but rather testifies and adds to it. Hence, *Faux Chic* draws your attention to the ways to combine furnishings from a wide range of styles and periods, focusing on the best each has to offer.

Faux Chic is also about comfort and intimacy expressed in both the arrangement and choice of furnishings, whether spare or froufrou, cluttered or pin straight, antique or modern. You and your guests will feel welcomed into a faux chic interior. You will feel cosseted in the space that uses ruffled curtains as a door—bohemian in style, perhaps, but altogether cozy chic. A kind of dialogue of histories, yours and the aesthetic languages of your furnishings, will stir conversation and insight. It will calm. It will give ease. Your home may feel light and airy like the corner of an industrial loft converted into a playful dining room á la urban chic, or you may feel ponderous and heavy like the living room filled with plump chairs and a sofa all dressed in rich textiles as in an English cottage. With the faux chic approach, your rooms will always feel embedded in a sense of history, particularly yours. It is this sense of warmth and personal presence that speaks in terms of a lived-in nonchalance that embodies chic style and that subliminally entices guests to make themselves at home.

In addition, *Faux Chic* will help you achieve a unique sense of space that is an extension of your own naturally evolving decorating sensibilities. As you pick and choose among the faux effects and embellishments offered herein, you will find yourself an unwitting sorcerer of rooms that speak in familiar tones through a surprising juxtaposition of shapes, color, and balance and that provide a setting in which the secret melodies of your soul resonate. You will find yourself in midst of the things you love—the furnishings, the collectibles, the clutter, the colors, the textures, and an unmistakable élan—and you will know that you are home like you are in no other place.

Ultimately, it is our hope, as authors, that you peruse the pages of *Faux Chic* and become impatient to apply the ideas you find in your own home. But remember, *Faux Chic* is not a rule book for you to slavishly copy the pictured interiors down to the last fleur-de-lis. Rather, it is a guide to using the illustrations, the information, and your creative imagination to create a chic home.

General information on selected faux effects has been provided and is noted with this icon. However, be sure to consult "Sources and Resources" on pages 139 to 141 for more detailed information that will help ensure professional-looking results and provide important working safeguards.

To support you along the way, *Faux Chic* concludes with an absolutely indispensable reference guide to finding the essential tools, materials, equipment, and decorative embellishments needed to create the faux effects and interiors featured in the collection. It also cites unconventional venues for finding quality furnishings, whether for purchase or inspiration. You will discover stores, both actual and virtual, for everything from stippling brushes to silk fringe. In addition, a list of authoritative works on faux effects is included should you desire more in-depth information. Above all, we hope you have fun, whether you choose simply to pin a tassel on a tablecloth, or to undertake the painting of an entire room. *Faux Chic* will be a trusted guide to help you find your own faux chic style.

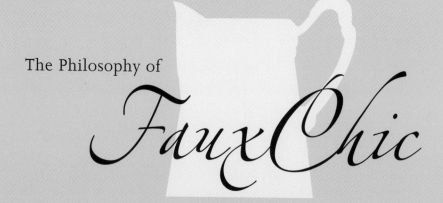

The Philosophy of *FauxChic*

BEFORE YOU START TRANSFORMING YOUR INTERIORS INTO FAUX CHIC environments, it is important to understand the underpinnings of chic style, whether it is described as bohemian, urban, dime store, European, English, or any other stylistic amalgam you can conjure. Faux chic is about emotion, not science, but it can be understood from the perspective of the few straightforward, albeit overlapping, guidelines. Stated simply, they are:

Follow your instincts, and choose what you love. Surround yourself with the things you love, using all five senses to make decisions about everything from arranging the furniture, to adding color to the walls, to placing your collectibles. Spend time in a room before adding anything new, assessing its personality and function. And by all means, remove anything that doesn't feel right for the way you live. Consignment and antique shops will welcome your castoffs. Most important, pay attention to your creative impulses as you go along. If you discover in some out-of-the-way flea market an irresistible table whose legs are a bit too wobbly to function as originally intended or some other "must have" hidden under a few decades of grime, get them anyway; simply be willing to enjoy them as they are in all their beauty or to restore them.

Choose quality overall. Most anchor pieces of furniture, like dining chairs, are meant to function and serve your lifestyle. Keep them in good repair, making certain they are structurally sound. Consider using a trained professional to remedy any problems that are beyond your ken. When a piece of furniture is out of tune with your tastes, consider altering it with a coat of paint, a swath of fabric, or a trim of some sort. Ultimately, a quality piece is always worth treating with a faux effect and incorporating into your decorating scheme.

Use what you have. Take a look at each room and decide which pieces are your favorites. Keep them. They carry a wealth of memories that make up your life experience. For the least-favored pieces, first assess their location in the room, and then rearrange them in unexpected ways;

sometimes placing them in a new context can revitalize your interest in them or show off their characteristics to greater advantage. You can add new life to pieces with a paint effect or surface embellishment. You will be surprised at how faux effects can transform an old piece into a different-looking piece that you fall in love with all over again.

Recast and recycle. Your choices should express who you are and how you live. That is exactly what faux chic is all about. If an inherited bedspread has exquisite handwork but doesn't serve your lifestyle, don't store it away, depriving yourself of so-enticing an item. Instead, use it in a different way: Drape it over an ornate curtain rod for an elegant window treatment, then add trim or a braided tassel as a tieback. Before buying brand-new pieces, check out flea markets and thrift stores, and recycle what you find. If a piece is structurally sound and has "good bones," apply a faux finish to give the piece fresh appeal. Often, you can find one-of-a-kind pieces that with a little effort and for a modest cost can be transformed into unique additions for your interior. What was once the metal grating around a sidewalk tree may now look great as the top of your living room coffee table, and a section of an upright piano that has been elaborately decorated with low-relief carvings may make an extraordinary headboard for the bed in your boudoir.

Take your time. Although the faux finishes and surface embellishments featured in this collection do not take a lot of time or money to create, don't rush through your home, trying to decorate everything at once. Feathering your nest is a process, unfolding over your lifetime in the large as well as small details. As you live in your space, you will reassess it often to suit your changing needs and resources. Allow your creativity to emerge. You will be rewarded with genuinely fine pieces and decorations that you will be proud to use and ultimately happy to pass down to the next generation.

Don't ignore the details. The personality of a room is revealed in the small details that articulate the many facets of your personality and the way you live. The term *faux chic* implies amiable clutter. Indulge your passions; they reveal the abundance of life. Inject your unique sense of style and personality into your interiors through layers of fabric, piles of books, tabletops crowded with little figurines, and the like. Don't hesitate to line up whatever you collect for all to see. For example, if you have 100 framed portraits scattered throughout the house, create a gallery on one wall to show them off. Statements like this can lift a room from being a box of impersonal stuff to the stuff of your trip through life.

Experiment. Be willing to try your hand at finishes and embellishments that appeal to your sense of style. Many faux techniques that have had daunting, centuries' old reputations for being difficult to achieve have been made fast and simple with the availability of modern methods and materials, and function-specific tools. For example, to add luxury to a junky-framed mirror, decorate the frame with a layer of gold leaf, an inexpensive metal sheet that can be applied with an adhesive. The gold leaf will illuminate the plain wood surfaces and create an elegant accessory for any room of the house.

Enjoy the process. Using faux finishes and effects to create a faux chic interior can be both fun and satisfying. The methods for aging new fabrics, antiquating just-purchased wood furniture, texturing walls, and embellishing flea market finds are very forgiving. It is likely that your first attempts at these faux techniques will be surprisingly easy ones, and you will be rewarded with professional-looking results, even if you are a beginner.

Don't mind the mess or the dust. Working with artists' tools and materials requires some preparation, and doing actual faux finishes can create temporary disorder in your home. After all, the creative process by its very nature is usually chaotic before it settles into a coherent statement that makes you sigh in admiration. But don't worry. Remember that the dust and neglect testifies to a passage of time, even if it is a contrived decade or two, so abandon your penchant for fastidiousness, and allow the faux chic style to settle in.

Improvise. Freedom to express your creativity is the key to inspiration, so relax and trust yourself to interpret your understanding of faux chic. You are in charge. Interpret the suggestions that are included as you see fit. And, by all means, improvise: Use a staple gun to put up a curtain, and drape your "best" plastic crystals over a chandelier. Trying out new ideas and taking a few shortcuts will give you that little bit of instant gratification that gets you through some projects and ushers you along in the projects that take a little longer.

ACKNOWLEDGMENTS

We wish to thank the following photographers, whose images illuminate the pages of this work: Guillaume de Laubier, Eric Roth, Steve Gross and Susan Daley, Steven Mays, Richard Felber, Rob Melnychuk, Mick Hales, Red Cover's Brian Harrison, Red Cover's Andreas von Einsiedel, Red Cover's Steve Dalton, Laura Ashley, Ltd., The Glidden Company, California Closets, and Shabby Chic.

We would also like to thank our publisher Winnie Prentiss, our editors Paula Munier and Stacey Ann Follin, our photo editor Betsy Gammons, and the staff at Rockport, without whose support this project would not have been possible.

The Dining Room

THE DINING ROOM PLAYS A VERY IMPORTANT ROLE IN THE SOCIAL LIFE OF YOUR HOME, whether you have a discrete space of grand proportions or a corner of a little room with a hand-me-down table and some chairs. Most important is that the dining space provides the atmosphere and comfort necessary for the nourishment, camaraderie, and celebration that transpires therein.

Assessing all elements in the room is key to transforming your dining space into one that allows you to express the hospitality and vitality that inspires extended stays around the table for deep conversation or hilarious fun. By evaluating architectural aspects like walls, floors, and ceilings as well as soft furnishings, lighting, and collectibles, you can coordinate your efforts to create schemes that not only are inviting and intimate but also bring out the character of the space. It is almost impossible to imagine decorating a space without the sweeping freedom of the faux chic approach.

General information on selected faux effects has been provided and is noted with this icon. However, be sure to consult "Sources and Resources" on pages 139 to 141 for more detailed information that will help ensure professional-looking results and provide important working safeguards.

Faux Effects for Architectural Elements

What is on the walls, underfoot, or overhead may rarely be observed at close range, but wall, floor, and ceiling designs usually continue the style message set up by the other interior features.

WALLS

When you enter a dining room, notice the walls. They delineate the borders of the actual space and provide a backdrop for all interior furnishings. When deciding what faux effects are compatible for the walls in your dining room, consider the number and placement of windows and doors. These architectural features determine the available wall space and introduce blocks of color, which need to be balanced with the rest of the furnishings. In all cases, you need to spend time in the room to decide which stylistic direction is most appealing to you. If the room is small, you can create the illusion of a larger space by leaving the walls white or making them a subdued color. If the room is large, on the other hand, or so cavernous that it is off-putting, you can make it feel more intimate by applying a darker color to the walls.

If the light in the room is generally more diffuse, you can lower the reflection by painting the walls a saturated color or one that absorbs the light and softens the glare. If the room appears dark or in the shadows most of the day, you may wish to apply lighter shades of paint to the walls, to enhance the light and make it bounce more. In all cases, when selecting your paint colors, examine them in both natural and artificial light. Brushing a sample of the paint over a section of wall is a fairly reliable test of how the color will play with and against the other interior design elements. Furniture and accessories will stand out or recede, depending on the amount of contrast between the walls and the furniture. However, choosing your wall color is an entirely personal matter. Just remember: The color should support the atmosphere you wish to create in the room.

FAUX PAINT EFFECTS

Faux paint effects are an easy way to achieve visual rhythm and texture on your walls. These techniques can provide shortcuts to recreating period finishes that reflect a particular place or age, or they can simply add depth and architectural interest to a room that has plain, flat walls.

A particularly foolproof category of faux painting is **colorwashing**, which is characterized by a broken color effect. It is achieved by applying a semitransparent glaze over an opaque base coat in a contrasting color and then texturing it with a paintbrush. The sweeping, crisscross action of the brush introduces fine gradations in color that give the wall a subtle texture and depth. The overall effect is one of shifting light and color, which simulates the period walls in English cottages, whose pigments were so unstable that they would naturally break down, creating the same colorwashed effect.

When choosing colors for your walls, you have a vast spectrum at your fingertips. Depending on your taste, you may opt for an obvious shimmering of color, in which case, analogous colors, such as yellow and orange, or those that are adjacent to one another on the color wheel are the way to go. For bolder contrast, use complementary colors, such as steel blue and ochre, as seen on the opposite page. By adding the darker blue pigment to the higher sections of the ochre walls, especially the borders and ceiling, the colorwashing has taken on an aged appearance.

Another foolproof paint effect is **faux striped wallpaper**. Stripes were the height of fashion in Federal-styled homes in America, and the effect is visually stunning. The stripes emphasize the height of the walls and create a visual rhythm that follows the architecture of the room. The process of creating the wallpaper involves placing parallel strips of tape at even intervals on a wall and painting over them using a roller. When the tape is removed, the base color of the wall itself is the color of one stripe; the alternating stripe is the second color that is applied between the strips of tape.

The gold coin-and-stripe pattern featured on page 31 is a variation in which circles are scribed on the wall using a compass and then colored gold using a composition gold leaf and gold size.

A thin layer of paint in flinty blue defines the edges of walls colorwashed a complementary ochre yellow. Primitive metalwork is evident in the flaming heart–shaped candle sconce, the adjacent brackets for hanging votives, and the wrought iron chandelier sporting strands of colorful beads. Portraits stare out from frameless canvases and overlook the stretch of a pickled-wood trestle table surrounded by painted ladder-back chairs. Their painted surfaces are decorated with primitive flowers, hand painted in a folk art style.

FAUX TEXTURAL EFFECTS

Looking to build up texture on a flat wall or change the stylistic character of its surface? There are several practical ways to do this. The effects depend on applying a new material either to the entire wall or to specific sections in order to cue in sensations of another place and time.

Textured plaster has a lively beauty that is created naturally by the effects of humidity, heat, and cold and the attendant expansion and contraction of the plaster. These occurrences produce interesting cracks and changes in the texture of the wall's surface, adding important historical and geographical references to your decorating scheme. A primary example are the houses and villas of the Mediterranean, whose walls are left to deteriorate.

ABOVE

The flickering candles in the ten-arm, painted chandelier and the votive candles on the distressed, drop-leaf table illuminate this intimate dining room, replete with crumbling plaster walls that have been left untouched. Mismatched wood side chairs with cutout designs on their splats are thickly painted different pale colors. By contrast, a majestic floor-to-ceiling armoire shows the original wood through progressively fading layers of paint, caused by aging and exposure to sunlight.

OPPOSITE

The striking effect of the red, gold, and green color combination is expressed in both the architecture and the soft furnishings of this dining area, providing a sense of lived-in luxury. The original plaster walls have degenerated over a century and show the succession of stains applied in bold gusts of terra-cotta, burnt orange, and light-brown paint. These colors stand in stark contrast to the white cracks that naturally occurred in the plaster and in the flaking paint on the ceiling beams.

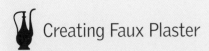

Creating Faux Plaster

Even if you have not enjoyed the benefit of inheriting a home with **distressed plaster walls**, you can recreate this look yourself and enjoy the rustic atmosphere of, say, a house in Brittany, where these effects occur naturally. The process of applying plaster to a wall requires effort and some expertise, but if you love the look, it is well worth trying.

- First, apply a base coat of paint to the wall.

- Then, rub clear paste wax on those spots where you want to see cracks and crumbling. The wax will resist the thin coat of wet plaster that you apply over the wall.

- After the plaster is dry, tap the waxed areas with a hammer and scuff them with a scraper and sandpaper. The plaster will break away from the waxed areas, creating the aged effects.

Plaster is one material that is receptive to color, making **tinted plaster walls** an ideal choice if you respond to the medieval characteristic of Italian frescoes. In the dining room featured below, washes of peachy terra-cotta paint tint ancient plaster walls. To replicate the look, follow these steps:

- Apply a tint, making it from an alkali-resistant powder pigment mixed in water with some white glue added as a binder.

- Then, apply the tint to sealed plaster walls using random brush strokes.

PAPER AND TEXTILE COVERINGS

Adorning your walls with pattern and color is easy when you use wallpaper and textiles. Although each material behaves differently and requires some expertise to put up, they look remarkably gorgeous in a dining room setting.

The appeal of traditional **wallpaper** is that it is available in an infinite number of patterns and colors for every budget, including wallpapers that depict faux painted finishes. Hanging prepasted paper makes for an easier job, and you can always consult a professional, if you prefer.

A wallpaper mural opens up a vista that enlarges the sense of space and atmosphere, giving a room depth it might otherwise not have. For a touch of romance and lushness, consider wallpaper reminiscent of *chinoiserie*, popularized by the French in the 1800s, as featured in the sweetly elegant dining room on the opposite page. This type of wallpaper print provides a number of decorating options for your walls. You can paper opposite walls in your dining room and paint the adjacent ones in a coordinating color or in

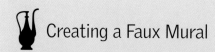

Creating a Faux Mural

An easy way to add the beauty of distant landscapes to your dining room is to create a faux mural.

- First, cut out single murals from the wallpaper, and apply them to a painted wall.

- Then, frame them with hand-painted garlands. Small hand-painted details can be achieved easily by combining stenciling with hand-painted details that extend the stenciled shapes farther onto the wall.

the same base color as the wallpaper. Then, you can use a combination of stenciling and hand painting to reproduce single design elements drawn from the wallpaper to decorate the monochromatic walls.

LEFT

Scenic murals and patterned wallpaper set up the romantic atmosphere in this dining *salon*. Above the dado rail is a muted expanse of louvered shutters, interrupted by oval murals delineated by leafy garlands. Imposing architectural elements are depicted below it. A restrained floral garland accents the marble tabletop, and single leaves form a border on the wide plank floor painted a faux marble. The painted chairs with backs constructed like lacy spider webs are naturally distressed from use.

OPPOSITE

A confection of color, this dining room is decorated with wallpaper inspired by the hand-painted *chinoiserie* of the 1800s. In a modern twist, tropical colors and motifs are lifted from the wallpaper and placed throughout the room—from the chair seats covered in fabric to the diaphanous silk panels hung on the window to the porcelain birds set out on the table. The saturated palette of the wall covering further distinguishes the sunburst mirror and the sensual silhouette of the marble fireplace in chocolate brown.

Decking the Walls with Textiles

Fabric opens up an expansive realm of possibilities for introducing a multiplicity of colors, prints, textures, and patinas—and for creating the design statement you are looking to make, be it subtle or bold. You can staple lengths of fabric to the wall at the edges, using an ordinary staple gun, each length butting up against the other. Then, you can conceal these stapled seams with piping or decorative molding.

The scrumptiously attired walls in the dining room on the opposite page illustrate how fabric can set the tone for an entire room—and you have a variety of sources from which to choose:

- First, seek out stores that sell to decorators in large quantities, because there usable lengths are left on large bolts, and they are less expensive to buy.

- Then, check flea markets and discount stores, as well as conventional fabric stores when sales are on.

- Also consider unconventional sources for materials, such as bedspreads and sheets.

ABOVE

A table runner in aubergine overprinted with an elegant embroidery pattern graces the full length of a dining room table. Ending in neat points at opposite ends, an otherwise plain cloth is made elegant by the cord-and-tassel detailing. Nearby place mats and napkins coordinate with the runner, as do the covered dining room chairs.

OPPOSITE

Swaths of ornately patterned fabric are pulled taut and secured to the walls in a minimally furnished dining room, creating a sense of visual clutter that belies the intrinsic order in the room. The fancy pattern of the wall covering is printed in raspberry on a cream ground. Echoing the colorway is a neat configuration of antique creamware serving pieces that almost recede into the textile pattern. A faux tile floor is rendered in a cream and café au lait diamond pattern. The ornate fireplace mantel and the painted chairs and table legs display the texture characteristic of a faux crackle finish. Bouquets of red roses and red cut-crystal stemware punctuate the central area of the table.

EMBELLISHMENTS

Small details can make powerful statements that add aesthetic value to an overall decorating scheme. Such is the case with decorative embellishments like moldings and carvings.

Moldings can successfully transform plain, flat walls into ones that have strong definition and depth, as seen in the dining room on the opposite page. Moldings of different widths and designs can be used to create a dado rail, faux recessed paneling, frames, and crown moldings that give dimension to your ceiling, baseboards, and so much more. You can configure simple open rectangles, nailing several to the wall in a neat row, or as you desire. You can paint the moldings in a color that matches or contrasts with the color on the walls. For a supply source of moldings worth looking at, check out architectural salvage firms or your local lumber and hardware store for various standard period moldings.

Once you have added moldings to the walls, you can capture some of the ambiance of an aristocratic interior by highlighting the details of the moldings in gold. Although transfer metal leaf is the standard material used to add gold detailing, you can simulate the same effect more quickly by applying 18K gold spray paint. You can reproduce the effect shown on the opposite page, where the contours of the wide panel molding have determined the positioning of the bands of gold, giving the illusion that the wide molding is made up of three different lengths when it is in reality only one.

Another approach to raising the luxe level in your dining room is to add **low-relief decorative carvings** to the walls or other architectural features in the room. Because carved-wood detailing tends to be expensive, it is advisable to use it judiciously where it will be seen and appreciated and where it will be architecturally appropriate. Motifs can be centered over door molding, or they can be used to decorate the mantel on a fireplace as featured on the opposite page. You can buy convincing copies of carved-wood detailing, such as garlands of roses and leaves with tendrils and ribbons, or you can buy less-expensive versions made from synthetic resins that are quite beautiful and rival their hand-carved counterparts. They can be easily adhered to flat and slightly curved surfaces with glue, and they can be colored using gold leaf, paint, or another faux finish effect.

OPPOSITE

The audacious red walls and the white of the fireplace mantel and ceiling relieve the snob appeal of this grand dining room, where decorative moldings and carved embellishments are used to provide textural interest and beauty. Set over the dado rail are moldings configured into tall rectangles that neatly partition the flat walls so they appear as recessed wood paneling; gilt-edged molding is used to form a second frame around an oil painting. A carved frieze across the mantel is accented on either side by floral garlands.

FLOORS

Floors can be made of many materials. Most commonly seen in dining rooms are wood and stone. Less common, but often seen in industrial or modern settings, are floors made from metals, such as steel, or cement. Yet, no matter what type of floor you have or want to create, each material carries its own pronounced sense of style and period.

Wood floors that are left to show their original grain and color are usually protected with a coat of polyurethane. When the boards are laid out in a particular pattern, such as herringbone or parquet, they introduce style and texture to the room. Even heavily marred wood floors can be left bare. The warmth and glowing patina of polished wood can also be used, especially when it reveals its previous history. Many old city lofts have original wood floors, which provide an industrial-strength chic factor that impacts the sensibility of the entire room, as seen in the dining room on page 35.

Patterning Wood Floors with Paint

The authentic stone floors featured in the dining rooms on pages 16 and 20 were made from kiln-fired terra-cotta and from black and oxblood glazed tiles, respectively. For a faux chic effect, you can replicate the **natural stone pattern** on a wood floor using paint.

- Simply map out your design using tape, and apply the paint in several coats to build up a low relief.

- To simulate the granular character and roughness of stone, mix sand into the paint before you apply it, or use any one of the many faux stone kits available in craft and hobby stores. The kits make achieving the faux stone look much faster and easier. Just be sure to follow the manufacturer's directions on the packaging.

Another way to give pattern and texture to a painted wood floor is to add a faux effect that suggests a soft furnishing, such as a **patterned area rug**. Not only is it amazingly resilient, it is also completely washable. To add a faux rug or two to your floor, follow these steps:

- Before you paint, remove any buildup of wax or grime on the floor.

- After that, paint your floor one color.

- Then, paint the borders of the rug, stenciling motifs such as leafy garlands within the borders and adding freehand details for more design flow.

(continued on opposite page)

COVERED FLOORS

Ostensibly the most versatile floor coverings are those you lay over the existing floor, regardless of its condition. **Area rugs** can add warmth, both to cold floors made of stone or tile and to the emotional quotient of the space. The ethnic richness of woven rugs from the Middle East can add pattern, geometric tension, and texture to a dining room. These rugs can evoke distant lands and exotic cultures, and they may even dictate the rest of the soft furnishings as seen on page 38.

Always an exciting find, the perfect rug can come from any one of a number of places. Search flea markets, thrift stores, and antique shops for ones with history and charm. Even rugs with worn areas from those that tread before you are worth having. If you have identified the kind of rug you love but it is simply out of your price range, look through discount stores for a more affordable replica.

If you opt for **wall-to-wall carpeting**, there is no need to feel that you are making an ordinary choice. The broadloom available today come in an infinite number of colors and patterns. Animal prints make a confident design statement and add personality to any room. On page 41, an expanse of a white faux fur, reminiscent of a leopard in winter, warms up an otherwise cool, all-white space in a beautiful and surprising way.

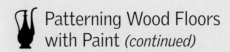

Patterning Wood Floors with Paint (continued)

Diamond and checkerboard patterns are popular choices for painted floors because they are easy to create, and they present a strong graphic component to your interior. Although typically seen in black and white, a subtle version of the diamond pattern in cream and café au lait is the perfect unobtrusive complement to the bold raspberry color featured on the walls in the dining room on page 24. The technique for creating the pattern is easy:

- Carefully calculate the amount of floor space you have, and scale the size of the diamonds to that measurement.
- Use tape to mark off lines, criss-crossing them to form diamonds.
- Use a roller to apply paint to the desired open areas.
- Be sure to seal the floor afterward to preserve the design.

If you are feeling a bit more ambitious, consider other shapes and colors, such as the octagonal pattern painted in cobalt blue on the floor of the dining area on the opposite page. Ultimately, keep in mind that your efforts do not have to be perfect—such is the charm of the faux chic approach.

OPPOSITE

This dining area maximizes the space in a larger room, yet establishes an intimacy. A Venetian blind and a metal exterior gate partition off the nearby kitchen. A row of sumptuous pillows camouflages a country bench pushed up against a wall that displays a precious collection of porcelain tureens overhead. Provençal cloth printed with exuberant swirls and acanthus leaves covers the long dining table, and a fun awning stripe is used to upholster formal side chairs. A repeat geometric pattern carries the room's colorway to the painted floor.

CEILINGS

Applying intricate faux effects to the ceiling is far less common because of the sheer physicality of decorating so large an expanse, and the scaling up one must do to make designs large enough to be noticed and interpreted from a normal floor stance. Traditionally, ceilings are painted white, but if you want to do something more interesting, consider adding painted or textured details overhead.

PAINTED CEILINGS

Although painting a ceiling white is a more traditional approach, it need not be boring. First, white paint comes in a number of shades, which gives you an opportunity to play with veils of reflected color. **Pure white** can act as a visual prelude to luxurious crown moldings painted white, or it can provide a contrasting canopy for walls painted a high-voltage color, making the wall color "pop." A **French vanilla white** on the ceiling can play a subliminal role in shifting the color of the room, adding a reflective glow to the adjacent walls.

TEXTURED CEILINGS

In all cases, however, it can't be denied that applying a faux effect to a ceiling can add amazing drama and atmosphere to a room. A ceiling with an interesting texture calls attention to itself and may even help to carry the stylistic theme of the room itself.

For an **exotic safari look**, consider embedding reeds into wet plaster that has been smoothed onto the ceiling, one section at a time, as seen on the opposite page. The reeds emphasize the use of natural materials expressed throughout the room, creating unified statement.

Many Provençal houses have heavy **ceiling beams** that actually bear the load of the upper floors. Consider adding beams to bring this rustic charm to your dining room, as seen on page 21. You can replicate the look using distressed beams made of lightweight polystyrene. The foam beams can be glued to the ceiling in approximately the same place that beams would run if the ones in your house were exposed.

OPPOSITE

In this safari-style interior, an exotic juxtaposition of natural tones, textures, and materials heightens the visual interest of the furnishings made from animal skin, distressed wood, and patinated metal. Walls painted in different faux patterns rim the unique reed-and-plaster ceiling. On one wall, a yellow-and-cream stripe is accented with metallic circles printed in gold paint. On an adjacent wall, uneven spots on a pale yellow ground create the witty effect of a faux cheetah pattern.

LEFT

This Venetian-styled sconce is made from mirrored sections of beveled glass and etched with simple flower-and-leaf designs. When the clear bulb in the holder is illuminated, its bright light reflects off each mirrored surface, creating a dazzling elegance in a room papered with period wallpaper depicting fragile tendrils and floral bouquets.

Lighting

Whether a glow of orange-yellow is cast from a nearby window at sunset or from candles set in a grand candelabra, changing light quality plays a significant role in setting the mood for chic style and intimacy. Light should relax the eye but also stimulate the imagination and encourage spontaneity. Balance light conditions by mixing up ambient light from artificial sources, such as lamps, sconces, and candles. If possible, install dimmers on electric lighting to modulate the intensity of the light.

Windows, in particular, determine the amount and quality of ambient light available in a room throughout the day. When you stand in your dining room, notice how light behaves. Strong afternoon sunlight that streams in through the windows may be mitigated by heavy drapes; translucent, light-filtering sheers; shades; or shutters. The dining room on page 35 is flooded with filtered daylight, giving the room enough natural brilliance to light up the spaces, as in the heavily draped window on page 39, which still allows light to fill the room through layers of gauzy fabric.

The flickering flames of **candles** provide a play of light and shadow, whether used alone, as in the style of the votives featured on page 20, or displayed in a towering candelabra or diminutive wall sconces. The appeal of candles is that they instantly transform a space into one that is theatrical and romantic. Placed on a table, they illuminate the rich detail in textured linens; they reflect light off glass surfaces such as cut-crystal goblets; they glow warmly on antique silver and china; and they bring up the grain of polished woods. With the strike of a match, a lit candle alone can set the chic tone in any dining room space.

Where you have strong architectural details, such as ceiling-hung chandeliers and wall sconces, lighting becomes easy to manipulate at will. Whether electric light or candlelight is used, it is common to lower the light in the dining room to establish a more intimate atmosphere. Lower light also softens the contours of the furnishings, giving the dining room dramatic depth and character.

Chandeliers and **sconces** come in an infinite variety of materials and styles. You can choose whatever you desire. Flea markets and tag sales can lead to some amazing finds at really reasonable cost—from chandeliers made from wrought iron to wood, glass, and crystal of every description. If you fall in love with an old chandelier that has irresistible line and style but whose surface condition is marred beyond restoration, get it anyway. If it doesn't light, convert it for candles. Then, hang it as a chic fixture with compelling textural pedigree.

If the chandelier you find is crystal or glass, dismantle it carefully, washing the glass sections in warm, soapy water and wiping them dry. Reassemble the chandelier, and hang it in an unexpected corner of the dining room, especially in a place that is backlit. The crystal facets will put on a glacial display of reflection. Continue to be on the lookout for mismatched crystals or glass beads of any color, adding them to the chandelier as you go along.

If your chandelier or sconce is made of metal, treat it with a patinating fluid like verdigris to add classical Greek flavor. Rich surface patinas add great decorative effect to a dining room interior. The wrought iron chandelier on page 19 echoes the rusticity of the metal sconces primitively cut from metal sheets, sending a strong note of western simplicity and style. The patina of brass sconces allowed to oxidize is spectacular when placed against a white wall. The deep orange-brown of rusted metal can coordinate with upholstery fabrics in a similar way. Although you can use the safer faux paint effects to simulate these surface states, the same metallic finishes can be achieved using kits that actually patinate the metal. Simply keep in mind that they may contain toxic chemicals and should be used with extreme caution.

 ## Transforming a Chandelier with Color

To quickly and easily change the style of a chandelier, use spray paint. The eighteenth-century carved-wood chandelier on page 20 was spray painted a creamy white. The color unites all the interesting design elements and changes the stylistic sensibility of the chandelier from serious to fanciful. Making the transformation is a snap:

- First, clean the chandelier, removing all visible dust and grime.

- Then, prime and undercoat the entire piece.

- Finally, add the topcoats of paint, always protecting the sockets and plug from overspray.

Furniture

Although the dining room requires only a table and chairs to function, it is one room where you can go overboard to express your chic style. The key to success in expressing your chic style is simply a matter of keeping **spatial relationships** and proportions in mind, and maximizing the use of the most interesting architectural features. A fireplace of any age can create a sense of welcome. It can serve as an elegant backdrop for a table placed nearby, where at such close proximity, you and your guests will be able to appreciate its particular history, style, and ornamentation.

Your dining room need not be of palatial proportions to make your guests feel cozy and feted, of course. Regardless of room size, you can establish a sense of camaraderie by the way you arrange the furniture. It can be charmingly crowded into a small space, but you must leave enough walkway between the pieces to allow guests unencumbered access. Remember that with little exception, the furniture and accessories are part of a moveable feast, so don't be shy about commandeering extra chairs to make room for guests or preparing a few sexy slipcovers to coordinate spare chairs that stand at the ready along the wall. The effects you add should work in tandem with the ceremonies you plan and the atmosphere you wish to create. And the pieces upon which you apply the techniques—whether a hand-me-down a few generations old or something brand-new—should have the line and structural soundness worth your efforts.

FAUX PAINT EFFECTS

Painting is one of the quickest and easiest ways to transform furniture made from wood, metal, wicker, or practically any other material. Whether you picked up an old armoire at a flea market or a few brand-new unfinished chairs, brush-on paints, spray paints, stains, and faux finishing kits are all readily available to help you transform them into items that will enhance your dining room atmosphere.

On page 16 a set of wooden chairs is painted a soft sage green. The color is accented by hand-painted detailing in white along the simple contours. The fun of painting wood is that the paint instantly transforms the look of the wood. The dining room chairs on page 19 have a folk art style, each slender line accented by primitive flowers hand painted in bright colors. If you need additional chairs to accommodate extra guests, buy a few spare chairs of mixed styling, and paint them either in one color or in a palette of soft pastels like those seen in the dining room on page 20. Just remember that before you begin to paint a hand-me-down chair, you should use a solvent to remove any grease and grime so that the paint adheres for a smooth finish.

OPPOSITE

A roomwide expanse of translucent fabric throws the geometry of these playful wood chairs into relief in this light-filled industrial space. Painted in grayed primary colors, the chairs have seat sections with metal joinery. A hospital gurney is the base for a polished plank of blond wood that serves as a tabletop. The crude ruts and gouges in the dark pine floor add character and warmth to the linearity of the scheme, and suggest a previous factory life.

 ## Staining Furniture—French Country Style

To introduce the soft, chalky colors like those found on the French country armoire in the dining room on page 20, begin with a piece of furniture made from untreated wood.

The "untreated" aspect is important because the wood needs to be porous to absorb the stain. Whether you are looking for an armoire, a chair, a buffet, or some other piece, you can go to any store that specializes in unfinished furniture to find just the right piece.

- First, wipe down the wood to remove any grease or grime before applying the colored glaze.

- Then, apply the stain over the wood, pushing the color into the curves and crevices, and wipe it off with a rag. The pigment will saturate the wood and leave a soft glow of color.

FAUX TEXTURAL EFFECTS

Nothing is more beautiful than the look of old dining room furniture with its historic nicks and scratches, and chipped and peeling paint—a testament to the use of generations before. Thankfully, new technology and faux finishing kits allow you to achieve this same heirloom feel without the wait. Suddenly, the wear and tear of weather and time can be sped up to achieve the same results.

Soft Furnishings

Using textiles in the dining room is a wonderful way to soften edges, emphasize comfort, and entice guests to your table. Accent chairs, tables, and windows with coordinating fabrics to add color, pattern, and texture to the room. You can buy chairs with extraordinary finishes and surface decoration that go well with satin, silk, and brocade fabrics. You can also introduce some stylistic irony by pairing a Queen Anne framed chair with a faux fur seat.

OPPOSITE

The stark white and black coloration disciplines the understated style of this dining area. An unassuming hutch is painted white, its contours picked out in black, along with the pillars that stand at opposite sides of the lower chest of drawers. An ornately framed mirror overlooks a bentwood table covered with a striped cloth. Framed lithographs line up across the wall. Pearl gray colors the walls and the floor, and "calf" length seat slips, naively sewn from a mix of pale blue and white patterned cottons, adorn the chairs.

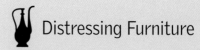

Distressing Furniture

PRESERVING OLD FURNITURE

If you are interested in preserving the rusticity of a distressed surface, one that is already nicked and scratched from real use, you can. To protect the finish and enjoy the rich grain, add a satin patina by waxing the surface:

- Apply paste wax in long strokes along the grain.
- Then, buff with a soft rag.

The drop-leaf table on page 16 shows the timeworn effects of use, preserved and polished, glowing under a coat of beeswax.

AGING NEW FURNITURE

You can ease new furniture into your decorating scheme by accelerating the effects of time on wood furniture and making it look stylistically old:

- Use fine steel wool to rub the edges of the back, seat, legs, and arms to simulate the distressed look that would result from years of use.
- Use cheesecloth to apply "grime" in the guise of burnt sienna or raw umber glaze to those areas that would naturally have caked-on dirt, like the dents and cuts in carved detailing.
- To simulate insect infestation, use a toothbrush dipped in brown glaze to spatter small flecks in a random pattern, or use an ice pick to create "wormholes." Use a paste wax to polish the painted wood and to bring up the contrast between the painted surface and the exposed natural wood.
- Finally, visit flea markets, tag sales, and architectural salvage houses to find ornate knobs and hinges, or apply faux finishes to new ones.

ABOVE

The drama and opulence of the Middle East is evoked in this dining area marked by a profusion of patterns that key off shades of rich madder red. An embroidered tablecloth spills from a tabletop to the floor below. The graceful motifs of the carpet are repeated in mother-of-pearl inlays that decorate matching side tables. Hand-painted patterns that resemble the intricate designs of metalwork and woven paisley decorate the matching book vaults that are separated by a wide seat covered in a bold graphic fabric.

OPPOSITE

Veranda chairs make a surprising showing next to a round table dressed bacchanalian style for an afternoon buffet. A classical statue of a child wearing a vine boa with flowers and fruit stands on layered linen and damask cloths pushed into soft folds. Diffusing the light from the window are yards and yards of gauze made into a classic swag accented by side rosettes. Opposing sheer panels drop gracefully from behind the swag and fall into pools on the floor.

WINDOW TREATMENTS

The decision to decorate windows is always an extension of style and privacy. If you like fussy window treatments that look like Balenciaga ball gowns, you will need some sewing talent. However, if you prefer a more nonchalant approach, you can use a few shortcuts to get the job done. **Floor-to-ceiling patterned sheers** are easy to hang by a pressure rod. They are lightweight, and they filter light well. You can drape several long swaths over the rods to create a Grecian effect like that featured on the opposite page. If you are looking for something a bit heavier and more formal, you can find **drapes** in heavy upholstery-weight fabrics to coordinate with the other soft furnishings in your room. Although these heavier drapes are more cumbersome to make because of the weight of the fabric, they are nonetheless technically straightforward: Lengths of fabric form panels that are either threaded on a rod or pinched into pleats and hung. The sage-and-white check curtains featured in the country French dining room on page 16 are subtly formalized with tiebacks.

CHAIRS AND SOFAS

When your family or friends gather around the table, you will want them to stay and enjoy the meal and the conversation. One key is to provide **comfortable seating**. Slide a couch up to the long side of a table for extracomfy seating, adding a pile of oversized European pillows on the seat to raise the diners to dining level. If your chairs have hard seats, add some soft cushioning by making a simple pillow. Use the contour of the seat surface as a pattern, cutting two identical pieces of fabric. Cotton velvets come in a wide range of colors and hold up well to wear and tear. If you have pillows that fit the seat, apply a tassel fringe to the seams, or stitch on faceted glass beads to each corner for extra glamour.

You can recover the seat of a wood-framed chair using a small amount of fabric and a staple gun. The seat base is already there; all you may need to do is remove the old fabric and use it as a pattern to cut the new fabric. If the fabric is missing, you can use the seat base as a pattern.

You can unify a set of mismatched chairs by quickly sewing **chair slips**, those loose-fitting skirts that soften the line of hardwood furniture. The chair seat slips on page 37 are custom fit to the chair seat. The long hem is sewn to the perimeter of the seat section. If you use washable cotton, you can antique the fabric by submerging it in tea or you can fade the colors by submerging it in a bleach bath. To reproduce the tattering and shredding characteristics of worn fabric, use rough sandpaper or a steel brush to fray the threads on the curved sections of the cushions or seat.

TABLE COVERINGS

In a well-appointed faux chic dining room, even a simple supper becomes a feast when the table is set with care.

Beginning with **linen**, atmosphere is easy to establish when you use color to coordinate the soft furnishings, from napkins and tablecloths to seat cushions. In the informal setting on the opposite page, patterned textiles play a role in establishing integrity of space in an interior whose dining area shares space in a larger room.

For a more formal setting, search tag sales and antique shops for vintage linen. Unused sets of intricately embroidered linen tablecloths and napkins are often available at low cost, primarily because of their high maintenance. However, there is little to compare to the French cutwork tablecloth that introduces a pristine sophistication well worth the laundering requirements.

For a casual chic table, drape several tablecloths in different styles on one table. Use yards of textured damask as a backdrop for a smaller cloth with embroidered cutwork and delicately curling monograms. Consider other textiles in the house that would make a unique tablecloth—a quilt, a bedspread, or even a sheer curtain. Or, if you want, you could leave the table bare.

Decorative Accessories

The accessories typically found in a dining room fit no particular category, except they are chosen because they have aesthetic and emotional meaning. The selections might appear frivolous to someone else, but to you, you can't imagine living without the **personal items** that give you so much pleasure—a lamp with a fringed silk shade, a tiny table that holds one silver frame, fine porcelain bowls that look out from a fireplace mantel.

Perhaps you inherited the last few unbroken pieces of Grandma's **china**, and you found mismatched **crystal** drinking glasses at a flea market and imitation pink depression glass bowls at a discount store—use them all together! Mixing and matching patterns and colors when setting your dining room table provides a venue for appreciating vintage pieces that have been separated from their sets.

CENTERPIECES

A collection of your favorite things, such as little porcelain figurines or teapots, can serve as a dynamic centerpiece for your table, as can leather-bound books and flowers. The ultimate harmony between outdoors and in is revealed in the **flowers** and **foliage** you harvest from your own garden or from a reputable florist. Botanicals, flowers, fruits, and vegetables look fabulous when piled to overflowing in large pedestal **urns** and wrapped like a boa around a classical statue as seen on page 39. Spring bulbs that bloom in the dining room bring the outdoors inside, as does setting **potted plants** on the table, arranging them in a narrow hedgerow down the center of the table. Compose a still life, lining up **bud vases** and placing a single stem of some exotic flower or herb in each one. Collect the vases together to create a garden effect. Use flowers in profusion, whether real and artificial. Load them into urns. Bundle them in **baskets**. Stand them in pots. Place them by an open window to stimulate their fragrance. Root avocado pits in your collection of **cut-crystal pots**. Place a slender stem of a poppy or sweet pea in a champagne flute or an armload of lilac in a widemouthed **apothecary jar**. When setting the table, consider using reflective surfaces like **mirrors** or glass under your centerpiece. The added bounce of light is romantic.

Collectibles

Whatever collectibles you have, display them where they can be used and where their details can be seen up close and appreciated. Move the **smaller collectibles** to new stages, giving them the same prominence as you would framed fine art. On page 23, a hand-painted porcelain figurine is featured as the centerpiece of the dining room table; on page 28, the unique beauty of the tureens is showcased on the open shelves in the dining room. Whether you find your special item wrapped in tissue and stored carefully, or you unearth your treasure in a box of junk, you will want to ensure that your heirlooms are here for the next generation to enjoy. Remember to keep precious items safe—set them away from the edge of display surfaces like mantels, tables, shelves, and windowsills, and keep them out of busy walkways in your home.

OPPOSITE

A combination teapot and teacup is paired to create this dainty tea-for-one service. Porcelain sets come in an exquisite variety of colors and patterns, and can be collected and displayed on shelves and tabletops where their unique contours and hand-painted details can be appreciated at close range.

ABOVE

The planes of this cool modern dining room are defined by modern classics. An oval slab of white marble on the pedestal table cuts through the space, and the signature curves of the Eames pedestal chairs cut through the ladder-style design of the room's partitioned doors. Warming up the space is a leopard-print rug and a stained-glass shade patterned in a sixties-style floral. A quintet of whimsical folk art dolls is the only decoration on the walls.

The Living Room

THE LIVING ROOM IS ONE OF THE MOST PUBLIC INTERIOR SPACES IN YOUR HOME AND thus is likely to be the site of your most spectacular decorating efforts. It is also the room in which your decorations can create a dramatically personal theater in which to welcome and entertain guests.

Fundamental to the convivial functioning of the living room is a suite of furnishings—minimally, a sofa and an armchair or two, a table that faces the seating group, and perhaps a side table for a lamp. The actual number of furnishings is based more on your style of entertaining than the dimensions of the room. Living rooms of cavernous proportions might contain only the barest essentials, yet firmly establish intimacy through lighting and the display of personal collectibles. Tiny living rooms can be filled to the rafters with furniture and accessories, and still provide a welcoming space for guests. What contributes most to an inviting atmosphere is the sense of unselfconscious personality and lavish welcome that the furnishings provide. They can be clustered within close proximity of one another, or they can be set widely apart—as long as your guests have access to one another and as long as there is space to use the pieces comfortably. Overall, you want the arrangement to have some semblance of functional coherency so that the social gatherings you plan in your living room fulfill your goals for camaraderie, sharing, and fun.

That said, there are a few important things to keep in mind when furnishing your living room. Key is the proportion and scale of the furniture to the size of the living room. If your living room is spacious, you may have the luxury of creating several seating areas, grouping graciously proportioned furniture of similarly styled pieces, or ones that are entirely independent in scheme. If your living room is small, it is more common to scale down the size and number of furnishings; however, given the faux chic approach, you should feel free to choose whatever it is that provides you with a fundamental sense of being at home.

Establishing that unique sense of home in today's living room is easy using the wide variety of effects that allow you to transform a table, recover a chair, or decorate a wall. You will look forward to recombining the pieces you have exiled to the far corners of other rooms, now that you can revitalize them or display them with all their imperfections.

Faux Effects for Architectural Elements

Applying faux effects to the fixed features in your living room is easy when you first consider the design statements integral to the basic furnishings—that is, the existing textiles, fibers, and hard materials used in and on your furniture. Begin by recycling and updating existing furniture to create an inviting seating area, then take steps to ensure that your walls, ceiling, and floor complement these choices and complete the total look of your room.

General information on selected faux effects has been provided and is noted with this icon. However, be sure to consult "Sources and Resources" on pages 139 to 141 for more detailed information that will help ensure professional-looking results and provide important working safeguards.

WALLS

FAUX PAINT EFFECTS

Selecting a particular paint effect for the walls, one of the most dominant architectural features in your living room, is an important part of the decorating process already begun with the selections of couch fabrics, window textiles, and floor coverings. When viewing the walls as a backdrop, consider that painting the room in a dark color will give the impression of a smaller space. Painting the walls a warm or light color will homogenize the other room elements of similar tone. And, painting the walls a cool color will make the room appear larger. With these very general principles in mind, consider the following faux effects using the paint colors of your choice.

Aging Colorwashed Walls

With aged colorwashing, you can artifically age a colorwashed wall by applying site-specific shadowing to simulate the appearance of dust and grime that would naturally accumulate over decades. The technique is easy: after the walls are color-washed, go back and apply darker tones of glaze to sections of the walls that would naturally collect dust and grime—that is, near the ceiling corners and where the walls meet. You can also achieve the broken color base coat by using a sponge instead of a brush to apply the color.

To create the aged colorwashed effect featured on page 42, sunny cadmium yellow and ochre are color washed onto the wall in several veils of diluted color. Then, a brown glaze is brushed along the ceiling and the corners of the room, calling cheerful attention to the ceiling in robin's egg blue.

The intense red of the limewashed and colorwashed plaster walls sets the tone for the boxy furniture set widely apart in this cavernous living room. The couch and chairs conceal their well-used condition, draped in a symphony of patterned reds—block prints, checks, stripes, solids, and plaids. The ornate top mantel displays a colorful woven textile and surmounts a stone block fireplace. Texture is carried out in the floor, configured with artfully laid stones separated by a grid of stone blocks. The green-glazed earthenware pot holding the boxwood is Provençal.

ABOVE

The wholly individualistic style of this living room is first observed in the figurative mural on the wall, which soon becomes an abstract in a passionate field of exotic materials. An antique fur throw in silver fox and chinchilla falls over the back of a brocade-covered couch. The sexy thirties-style bedroom chair is upholstered in a leafy print that looks like an animal print from afar. A formal French-style chair is upholstered in traditional diamond-patterned damask and holds an animal print pillow, too small to provide anything more than visual appeal. The lacy design of the cast iron tabletop was originally the protective base laid around an urban sidewalk tree. Painted window moldings are stripped back to the original wood.

CHOOSING COLORS

You may wish to avoid using traditionally cooler colors like blue and green on the walls of your living room, preferring instead to impart a warm glow to the room. On page 54, the bright yellow of a high-ceilinged living room provides a soft backdrop for the painted furniture and delicate furnishings placed carefully therein. Flooded with light during the day, the same living room is still bright and cheerful at night, illuminated by lamps and candles. If your tastes run more to the formality of **cooler colors**, however, look at the living room pictured on the bottom of page 52, whose sense of clean lines and openness is the result of applying a moss green to the walls and white to the moldings.

White walls can also be dramatic counterpoints to furniture with visual weight. After all, white paint comes in an extraordinary variety of shades, from grayed-out whites to creamy whites that glow to dispassionately stark shades of ice and snow. The living rooms on pages 52 (top), 55, and 64 illustrate the power of white. However, you might also wish to add dimension to flat white walls by adding a pale tinted glaze to one or more walls in the room. You can use the colorwashing technique mentioned above, brushing on

ABOVE

A kaleidoscope of color is offered everywhere in this free-spirited living room with an American West sensibility. Beginning with the modern painting whose canvas is cross-sectioned into the colors of sky and clay, and continuing to the striped cotton pillows and the strong geometric of the dhurries on the modern sofa, the room is lighthearted and fun. A kitschy lamp sporting a cowboy shade is propped on a stack of magazines. A painted bench with chipped and peeling paint settles on a woven striped carpet reminiscent of western textile weaving.

 Creating a Mural

Adding a wall mural to a plain wall is a great way to incorporate the faux chic style into a room. Not only does it bring drama and depth to a wall, but it also serves as a wonderful conversation piece. If the idea of having a masterpiece on your wall is compelling, you may wish to consult a professional painter or a tromp l'oeil artist to help carry the idea through. The principle behind the technique is simple:

- Select your art from books or posters.

- Use a ruler and pencil to overlay a grid pattern on the illustration.

- Transfer the grid onto the wall with chalk, scaling up the sections so the proportions fit the chosen space.

- Copy the basic lines of the artwork onto the wall, sketching in details as desired.

- Use a paintbrush and acrylic paint to fill in the shapes, referring to the original art for guidance.

a transparent glaze in the palest French vanilla. The added veil of color will warm up the base color without being obtrusive or overly sweet.

If you choose to let your **artwork** set the style and colorway for your living room, look no farther than the room on page 46, where a pair of feet and a hand have been hand painted on adjacent walls, which are painted the color of sand. In the style of the Renaissance figure drawings, the rendering adds a sense of history to the room, while playing off the exuberantly patterned furnishings, whose colorway is infused with warm earth tones. If the idea of having a masterpiece on your wall is compelling, you may wish to consult a professional painter or a trompe l'oeil artist to help carry the idea through.

FAUX TEXTURAL EFFECTS

Giving your walls a textural effect is another way of giving a flat surface added dimension or a low-relief pattern, while evoking the wall surfaces of faraway places.

One effect that provides the geographic sensibility of places that enjoy hot climates is a **faux plaster** look. Actual plasterwork involves the constructional integrity of the wall, whereas creating the faux plaster effect involves applying a thin veneer of plaster over an existing wall to simulate the real thing. The plaster is applied to the wallboard previously sealed with two coats of paint. Although the plaster is smoothed as evenly as possible, keep in mind that pits and bumps are an unavoidable but charming characteristic of provincial plaster.

The European rusticity of the living room on page 45 shows an original plaster wall that has been colorwashed several times using veils of intense red pigment and then rubbed down using a rag dampened in denatured alcohol, a technique called **limewashing**. The paint-removal process artificially mottles the ground color, simulating the flaky texture associated with damp plaster walls. If you choose

to limewash your walls, it is extremely important to work in a well-ventilated room. When you are done, coordinate the resulting surface texture with a medley of soft furnishings that have an equally rustic style. In the living room mentioned above, the cotton textiles are dyed a wide range of rich reds and browns, appearing in bold graphic patterns that mix American checks with western tent stripes and a hand-blocked pattern configured into a decorative brickwork pattern.

White walls provide a neutral backdrop for **fine art**. Sometimes, the entire design scheme of a room is linked to a single piece of wall art, with the walls functioning simply as architectural support. A wall-sized abstract painting dictates the predominant colorway used in the living room shown on page 47. The original painting is done on a canvas cross-sectioned into large blocks of color, mostly the shades of sky, clay, and soil—colors associated with the Santa Fe region of the United States. The colorway symbolizes the geography of the West, and it predominates in the rustic furnishings, especially the dhurries and colorful blankets that cover the sofa, and the kitschy lamp shade depicting a cowboy.

If using a single piece of art provides a powerful statement, so does paving the walls with artwork of every description. The living room on the opposite page becomes a majestic gallery of **framed drawings and paintings**, together with shelves of books that make the eye rise to the ceiling where the last pictures are hung. In the featured

OPPOSITE

A dramatic sweep of framed art and books decorates the majestic wall that rises up to a roomwide arch at the ceiling level. Unhung paintings stand propped against the wall. Laid over the sisal carpet is a woven rug with a plaid border that defines the entertainment area. A functional mix of fine contemporary and period furniture provides an eclectic grace, with an upholstered camel saddle adding a stylistic counterpoint.

Embellishing with Molding

Adding structural features to the wall can add a sense of period style to your living room. Using decorative molding to set up a stylistic relationship between two rooms, especially the living room—dining room area typical of some apartment dwellings, will both unify and distinguish each space. For aristocratic elegance, copy the effect shown on page 27 on the walls of your living room.

- Frame out the walls on each side of a fireplace by joining strips of molding into rectangular frames and nailing them to opposite sides of the fireplace over the mantel.

- Rim the interior edge of the molding with plastic beading, which is sold by the yard in craft stores. When the entire wall, including the beaded moldings, is painted, the frames will appear to be integral to the walls, evoking the recessed paneling of English manor houses.

OPPOSITE

Central to the strong personality of this living room is the carved marble fireplace, daringly painted in a fantasy animal print resembling tiger fur. The warm golds and browns predominate the field, and the black splotches add accent. A bare bulb on a jointed-limb desk lamp lights the black frame with a gilt egg-and-leaf motif surrounding a pen-and-ink wash. Sharing the same wall are regimental rows of framed black-and-white photographs of American Indians matted in warm gray.

living room, several rows of framed art appear to be hung in a premeditated fashion, whereas many pieces appear to have been hung as acquired. Even if you do not have a wall full of art, you can still use art to add stylistic gravity to your interior. Uncluttered rows of framed portraits can flank a central mirror as in the living room featured on the opposite page, or they can be propped against a wall if you run out of inspiration or wall space.

FIREPLACE MANTELS

It makes sense to maximize the beauty and function of the architectural elements that lend decorating gravity, especially **fireplaces**. If you have one, consider arranging your furnishings according to their relationship to the fireplace. A fireplace instantly communicates warmth, and it can be the fixed point around which all furnishings are placed.

If your fireplace is plain-Jane, perk it up by painting it one color. The color can blend with the walls, or more interestingly, it can carry out the colorway of other furnishings in the room. On the bottom of page 52 the fireplace is painted black, as are specific pieces of wood furniture. In this way, color is used to unite the design elements and to call attention to the interesting lines of the chairs and the table.

With amazing individuality and creative flair, the marble fireplace on the opposite page is painted in an animal print pattern. To get the effect, the mantel was first painted a warm honey brown. Then, splotches of black paint were added to create a convincing fur texture. If you are interested in replicating a fur pattern, try to work from a sample or picture that shows the design. Or, use your imagination to create a fantasy fur of your own design and colorway. One cautionary note: When you apply paint to stone, the effect is usually permanent.

RIGHT

A surprisingly small living room shares its airy space with a home office featuring a desk bordered by tall windows that expand the room's visual reach to an outdoor garden with a pretty trellis. Sheaths of translucent fabric filter the light from the large windows, and lengths of the same fabric form light-filtering hammocks across the ceiling. The white furniture is functional and fits gently within its overall modern style, completing the cool order and airiness of an all-white room.

RIGHT

The wide-board floor painted to a glossy white echoes the pure white cotton of the cushioned seating in this long room. A painted fireplace has a robust hearth decorated with a cast-iron fireback that introduces a black palette, which unifies the minimal furniture—plain tables with spindly legs, a rattan chair, and a drum-shaped, leather ottoman. A stack of old leather suitcases serves as a convenient lamp table and is placed next to a freestanding wardrobe with satiny-smooth paneled doors painted black.

FLOORS

COVERED FLOORS

Floor coverings play an important part in living room decor because they help delineate the boundaries of seating areas or create divisions between seating areas, thus transforming even the largest of spaces into wonderfully intimate settings. So, naturally, one of the most common ways to treat a chic-style floor is to add a rug.

Easy to add and to move around, **wool area rugs** in rich patterns are divine underfoot, and they communicate a sense of historical elegance. A rug made in a sculpted pattern, like *Aubusson*, provides a tactile sensory experience that makes a living room extra cozy. The carpets in the living rooms on pages 54 and 60 are inherited, but good reproductions of old patterns are available in most carpet stores.

Wall-to-wall carpeting can also be used to cover floors in the living room. You can then break up the color of the carpeting by laying down a rug of a completely different style. On page 63, an elegant rug in a pattern reminiscent of French needlepoint is laid over a sisal wall-to-wall carpet.

CEILINGS

The living room ceiling is often thought about last because the traditional white ceiling works so well. However, you can add a heavenly glow to your ceiling by suspending independent **swaths of fabric**, hammock-style, across the ceiling as shown at the top of the opposite page. When a low light is turned on from above, the fabric glows.

Painting Floors

White is a terrifically chic choice for a wood floor that needs to be revitalized because the color immediately delineates the other design elements and furnishings that are placed on it. Painting a wood floor is easy, but it does require some advance preparation:

- First, empty the space of furniture, if you can.
- Then, clean the floor of any dust, grime, or grease so that the paint goes on evenly.
- Use a brush to apply the paint, allowing the paint to dry between coats.
- Finish the surface with a coat or two of protective polyurethane.

Decking the Ceilings with Textiles

A tented ceiling can add an exotic flair to a room by creating an Arabian Night atmosphere, and it can help cover a damaged ceiling. To integrate this faux chic look into your home, start with one swath of fabric at a time:

- Suspend wood dowels on opposite sides of the ceiling, using eye hooks and nylon cord to secure them.
- Then, measure the width of the ceiling, and use that measurement to determine the length of the fabric that you will drape.
- Repeat the steps if you wish to add more swaths.

Lighting

Light plays a dramatic role in the living room in many ways. Although the room is typically associated with evening entertainment and spaces glowing with electric light, the room can be a wonderful haven for you and your family during daylight hours. When natural light illuminates the furniture and accessories, your living room can become a sanctuary to relax and reflect or curl up with a good book. In the living room below, tall windows let afternoon light stream into the room. By contrast, only low light filters through the windows in an all-white room, based on its orientation to the sun, featured on the opposite page.

Candles can be placed in candlesticks, or they can be placed in a candelabra, Liberace-style. The value of the candelabra is that it provides a spectrum of light in a convenient, portable base. On page 57, a five-arm candelabra creates a romantic atmosphere that enhances the intimacy of the living room. On the opposite page, a wooden chandelier is fitted with candles.

There are many styles of **chandeliers**, each defined by the material from which it is made. Equal parts sculpture and lighting source, a chandelier can harmonize with the rest of the interior, or it can introduce a unique style in counterpoint to the style of the furnishings in the room. One of the most elegant chandeliers—and probably the most common—is made from lead crystal. A crystal chandelier appears glacial when lit at night and is most stunning when sunlight pierces the facets of each crystal in the day. For a decorative globe-style chandelier, see the open-cage design on page 42.

To recreate the look of peeling paint on a metal fixture or candlestick, you can begin afresh with a new metal, applying a series of patinating fluids. To avoid using the highly toxic chemicals that are common to this technique, use a mixture of latex paint, denatured alcohol, and whiting. When the ingredients are mixed, they form a paste, which you can apply to the object. After the paste has dried, wipe some of it away from the raised surfaces to expose the original color of the substrate. The nooks and crevices will retain the faux effect of the patinated and aged textures. To recreate the look of weathered copper in a verdigris color, use a sequence of colored pastes in light blue, mint green, and forest green. Although this finish naturally occurs on metal over time, its faux finish counterpart can be achieved on practically any material—for example, wood, plastic, or plaster.

LEFT

Tall, narrow windows flood this sophisticated yet intimate living room with sunshine. Its walls are painted a soft, lemony yellow, forming a backdrop for a degraded mercury mirror that is partitioned with beaded gilt molding. The room is filled with an elegant jumble of period pieces that have fine lines and interesting decorative detailing. The painted frame of the sofa is chipped, its gracefully curving back accented with a rose carving. Needlepoint pillows lay on its delicate ticking, designed with bursts of sweet william. Family photos and favorite collectibles in porcelain, crystal, and silver are scattered on nearby tables.

Supplying a subtler source of spot lighting, **sconces** are available in pairs and in a wide variety of styles. On page 60, a pair of wood-backed sconces is painted in folk art colors. On page 64, patinated metal wall sconces with fancy metalwork decorate the sides of a beveled mirror of the same century. You can even find sconces at bargain prices at flea markets, and you can substitute votive candles in small crystal cups for light bulbs if the electrical wiring happens not to work.

Lamps are made up of two interesting components: a base and a shade. Both are available in various styles, allowing you to express your chic style in ways that are compatible with your personality. Many antique shops sell lamp bases, long parted from their shades. If you find a great base, buy a plain shade and add decorations like silk fringe or beads. Great sources for these decorations are antique stores that sell old gowns and clothing. You can sew on the silk fringe or use fabric glue. Beaded fringe is available by the yard and can be hand stitched or glued to the shade. The mandarin-style lampshade on page 8 is a stunning accessory that repeats the elegant notes in this stylish living room.

ABOVE

The premeditated symmetry of this room begins with two deep-sill windows, separated by two framed works of art that take up the entire width of the rear wall. Afternoon light bleaches out the exuberant bouquets of dried foliage placed in a pair of iron urns perched on simple pedestals. The strong curves of the couch back outline the all-white upholstery and soften the restrained linearity of the interior. An imposing, heavy-armed chandelier carries black candles and hovers over a glass-top table, which displays nesting marble plates, tall glass odalisques, and a curiously placed magnifying glass.

 ## Recreating the Look of Peeling Paint on Wood

Just as you can create the look of peeling paint on metal, you can create the same effect on wood, using a slightly different technique:

- Apply a light coat of grease on the painted wood surface.

- Then, apply a second coat of paint in a contrasting color.

- After the paint has dried, use sandpaper to gently remove the blistered paint, exposing the paint beneath. The paint will appear grotty and crumbly in sections, but these effects are part of the look.

Furniture

In the faux chic living room, furniture choices are made foremost with comfort in mind. The living room should be physically comfortable with the sofa and chairs begging you to sink into them. Minimally, a living room should emit a sense of lived-in comfort that appeals to the emotions, even if the furniture is expensive, absolutely ancient, or painstakingly dainty.

FAUX PAINT EFFECTS

If you want to unite many different furnishings in your living room, use **one color** of paint to coalesce them. When painted furniture is placed around a room, the common color draws the eye from one form and surface to another. The shabby chic living room on page 64 is a perfect case in point. The white paint conceals the grime and age of the wood and metal surfaces it covers, but it also brings out the graceful shapes and the rich textural details of each painted item, including frames and a degraded mercury mirror flanked by the metal grillwork above the mantel. For more drama, use bold, **contrasting colors**. Pair white with black. Use black paint on hardwood furniture, even if the pieces are dissimilar in style, and apply the same paint to the architectural elements, like the fireplace mantel and the hearth as seen at the bottom of page 52.

OPPOSITE

An incongruous day bed serves as conventional seating in this French living room with tall shuttered windows. Placed in front of an imposing stone fireplace with carved frieze, the opposing carved wood headboards of the seating have slender fluted columns that end in acorn finials. The French-style daybed is upholstered in a traditional mattress ticking that covers the bed components and dresses the tall shuttered window. Throw pillows in a bright marine blue are accented with squares configured in white bands.

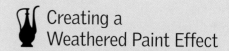

Creating a Weathered Paint Effect

When a painted surface is exposed to the elements, the paint buckles unevenly, revealing any other colors that were applied before. To achieve the look of weathered paint, examine the rococo candlesticks and frames in the living room on page 42, which show the effects of moisture on painted layers. The buildup of moisture under the painted layers undermines the adhesion of the white paint meant to cover them. The following steps will help you simulate the effect:

- Paint the wood, and allow it to dry.
- Then, wet it until you see the paint buckle.
- Use a dry brush to nudge off some buckled paint.
- Then, wipe down the piece, and let the paint dry.

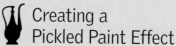

Creating a Pickled Paint Effect

Paint can also be used to stain natural wood so that it resembles pickled pine. With the subtraction method, white paint is applied to an unfinished wood item and then wiped off, leaving the stain deep in the wood. The daybed in the living room on the opposite page has the beautiful ghosting of white color characteristic of pickling, as does the living room sofa featured on page 42. This same effect is also attractive on architectural elements, such as window moldings and doors, as seen in the same living room. Applying glaze in colors is an alternative to using white paint. The result is one of soft, faded color and age.

Soft Furnishings
WINDOW TREATMENTS

For spaces that are more sophisticated and fancy, you can add a touch of humor to the style by introducing a bold graphic pattern in the window treatments. The red-and-cream striped **shade** on the opposite page presents a playful counterpoint to the stately period furnishings in the same living room, as do the formally styled **drapes** made of common ticking fabric normally used on bare mattresses, as shown on the daybed on page 57. The light-hearted sensibility of each window treatment relieves the room of its more formal, self-important feel.

Of course, if you want to carry out the formal feel of the more sophisticated pieces, do so. There is something majestic about capping a ceiling-high window with a scallop-shaped billow of silk, as featured on page 54. The valance dresses up the window, while leaving the narrow windows free from encumbrance so that light can enter the room. For a more sumptuous elegance, hang drapes that match or contrast the color of the walls, as shown on page 63, or to ensure additional privacy or to delineate one space from another, hang embroidered panels of lightweight silk.

OPPOSITE

The graphic red-and-cream awning stripe on this window shade strikes a fun note in the corner of an elegant living room. A small marble mantel is converted into a console table, its shelf a promontory for a pair of brass lamps with shiny red shades and an exquisite five-arm candelabra with a cut-crystal base and gilded metal arms topped with lustrous oval shades in jewel tones. Delicate branches with leaves and crystal flowers extend into a spray above and behind the oval shades. Sheltered at the base of the table is a thirties-style mirror with a mitered frame, which reflects back the luscious ruby red color of a nearby couch.

CHAIRS AND SOFAS

If your furniture is a bit rattier than you would like it to be, you can add fresh color and style by covering the item in a textile. You can drape patterned blankets or carpets over chairs and sofas not only to conceal worn areas but also to provide colorful accents.

Any textile you find and love can be transformed into **loose covers** for your furniture. Dhurries can be slipped off the floor and laid over a couch, as in the living room featured on page 47, or they can be configured from wide swaths of cotton or velvet laid over furniture like a huge bedspread. On page 45, a multiplicity of patterned cottons expressed in bright red and white are placed over the boxy furniture, imparting a casual air to a stately, centuries-old interior. Drape yards and yards of a richly textured fabric on a sofa or chair, tucking the fabric between the cushions. Heavy

Re-covering an Ottoman

Using the same principle as you do when re-covering a chair seat, you can also change the fabric covering on an ottoman.

- Use the seat measurements plus a hem measurement to create a cover for the seat section.

- Then, use a common staple gun to secure the fabric to the wood.

- Finally, position upholstery tacks in an even row around the perimeter, or arrange them in more intricate designs to add curves and angles to the line of the piece. To maintain period consistency, consider antiquing the tacks using a tinted glaze.

Decorating with Slipcovers

If you can **sew**, you can make slipcovers for all or some of your upholstered furniture. These covers are ideal because you can simply remove them when it is time for cleaning or laundering.

An option to sewing slipcovers is to **buy** them ready-made from one of the many home and discount stores that carry them. The slipcover may not be perfect fit—but then again, with the faux chic approach, it does not have to be. Slipcovers can be plain and simple, or they can be so detailed that they arrest the eye and change the sensibility. Big ruffles, for example, add a romantic touch, whereas a pom-pom fringe can strike a humorous note. Also, floral prints with overblown roses look beautiful on big couches. To dress up your slipcover up a bit, you can add fringe or tassels; a little hand stitching and fabric glue will do the trick. You can also simulate the effects of wear and fading:

- If you are making your slipcover, wash the fabric before you sew it to preshrink it, to remove the size, and to soften the fibers; if you are using a ready-made one, simply wash it.

- Then, use bleach to tone down saturated dyes, or age the fabric by submerging it in a tea or coffee solution.

upholstery-grade cotton twill is sturdy, and looks attractive on overstuffed sofas and chairs with rolled arms and big, loose pillows. Use flowing **scarves** on upholstered furniture as on the opposite page, draping several over the arm of a chair or wherever you want a splash of color. For added sparkle, sew crystal beads on the hem to make a fringe, or add faceted buttons for accent. A mixture of old and new textiles like those seen on page 42 creates a deceiving but luxurious clutter of pattern, color, and texture on the furniture in this room. For added flair, attach a tassel to each corner of the blanket, carpet, or fabric.

TABLE COVERINGS

For tables that are often used for entertaining, you might consider adding sensual fabrics to romanticize them. Drape an embroidered **shawl** on a coffee table. Crisscross lengths of hand-crocheted **runners** on a long table. For side tables and mantels, lay down hand-crocheted lace **doilies** or vintage handkerchiefs with printed designs.

THROWS

Combining various textiles in one interior is a great way to add a touch of drama to a living room. Although any fabric you gravitate toward is the right choice for you, no living room would be faux chic without a **fake fur throw**. Because plush fabrics with fake fur patterns are so abundantly available, you can choose among zebras, tigers, leopards, cows, and fantasy prints that add vitality when turned into fashionable lap throws. You can sew two large rectangles of fake fur together, adding big tassels or fringe for glamour.

OPPOSITE

A multiplicity of heavy textiles saturated with color and pattern provide the stylistic muscle in this companionable living room. Fringed runners and lap blankets conceal the thread-worn areas of a velvet wingback chair and drape the seat of a stout chair dressed in a striped damask. An upholstered, ottoman-style table stands in front of an Empire-style couch, elongated by its upholstered, multicolored horizontal stripe. A jumble of velvet pillows punctuates the stripes. An urn stands sentry on a painted column, now chipped and peeling. A beautiful candle sconce looks like a torch painted in gold leaf and Russian folk art colors.

PILLOWS

Pillows can serve a living room in many ways. They can introduce hits of bold color and pattern as they do in the living room on page 60. Or, as in the Southwest-styled living room on page 47, they can help carry out the colorway of a room, while creating visual interest through the use of pattern; although the dhurrie on the floor brings in yet another pattern, it stays true to the colorway of the room.

Surprising, but true, you don't need to sew to make a pillow. If you want to **accent** existing pillows, consider adding trims using fabric glue or a hot glue gun. Cord and tassel tiebacks can be tied around a pillow, creating the look of a wrapped package. Lace doilies can also be affixed to pillows, as can silk flowers or costume jewelry. Anything is possible when you use your imagination.

To create a new, **no-sew** pillow, you can use vintage embroidered handkerchiefs, soft silk squares, or even store-bought scarves to make a case for a pillow form, just by tying the pairs of ends together at the corners. To **recycle** an old

sweater, slip a pillow form into a boiled wool sweater that you may have outgrown or accidentally washed, crossing the sleeves and securing them with a big brooch. Still, another option is to weave wide ribbons, basket style, and tie them where the ends meet.

Pillows can also simultaneously serve as art, as in the **needlepoint** pillows featured on page 54, which add floral designs and personal mottos to a formal yet elegantly comfortable couch. If you don't do needlepoint yourself, flea markets, estate sales, and your grandmother's attic are good places to find aged pieces that would have been readily available for former generations. If you sew, you can make more intricately styled pillows. But simple sewing is all that is required to back the needlepoint with fabric, thus creating a slipcase for an inexpensive store-bought pillow. These can be accented with ribbon, trims, or fringe, as you desire. When sewing pillowcases, keep in mind that if you add a zipper, you will be able to remove the pillow for easy cleaning or laundering.

LEFT

A romantic stack of pillows in a variety of shapes and sizes can be piled onto a couch for a sumptuous seat. For subtle harmony, choose those made in similar colors but in distinctly different patterns and weaves to create a dynamic impact.

Decorative Accessories

After you have treated the larger elements of your living room to your particular faux chic efforts, continue to add accessories to further add personality and
character. Accessories tend to have more visual weight and a designated function. They take the shape of mirrors, framed art, or any inanimate objects that
coalesce with your decorative intuitions. However, accessories can be natural
flora and fauna, like live topiary, tropical fish, and caged birds, if you so desire.
Flowers, of course, are an old standard that never fail to satisfy the eye and coordinate with the spirit.

ABOVE

The bold contrast between the gold and berry
plays itself out in this richly appointed living
room. The gold of the painted walls harmonizes
with the plump two-seater sofa and balances
out the rich berry textiles used on the large
sofa and the floor-to-ceiling drapes. A glass-top
coffee table opens up the center space and
introduces a curvilinear design, also found on
the end tables and console table.

RIGHT

White dominates the colorway in this living room, yet it belies the rich surface textures that decorate the furnishings on closer inspection. A plump chair and a sofa with an oversized ruffle are reflected in a antique beveled mirror, decorated with carved details painted white. Flanked by ventilation grillwork and French-style crystal sconces, the room is bright during the day and lit by a glacial beauty of the central chandelier at night. The weathered mantel displays a chipped ceramic pot filled with white roses.

MIRRORS

Mirrors are fabulously versatile accessories in that they can add dramatic accent to a wall and enlarge the visual space in a room. The partitioned mirror on page 54 is magnificent, reflecting the soft light and delicate lines of the interior furnishings. Although reproducing a mirror of this size and style is a daunting task even for a professional, you can simulate the look in a smaller version by using a special spray paint, available at craft and hobby stores, that simulates the reflective depth of a mirror. In a snap, you can transfer a piece of **beveled** glass into a mirrored surface. Once the glass has been painted, fit it with a wide, sculpted-wood frame, accented with any faux finish of your choosing— aging paint, crackle, or gold leaf.

FRAMES

Frames made from any material can be treated to a faux finish. Although **wood** frames are the most common, ones made from **plastic** or **metal** can be accented just as easily. The decorated frame hanging over the mantel on page 51 is characterized by a highly polished black finish, together with the soft glow of applied gold leaf. Treating wood frames with **gold leaf** is one way to achieve the effect, whereas spray painting with authentic 18K gold is usually quicker if you are covering a larger surface area. If the regal warmth of gold does not suit your decor, metal leaf is also available in silver and copper, as are brush-on and spray paints.

FINE ART

If you are looking for a great **art sources**, search out old books that contain engraved plates. Although technically not as valuable as the originals, framed **prints** can add character and personality to your walls. Museums are another wonderful place to buy copies of well-known artwork, both in poster size to fill the space on a large wall over a couch, for instance, and in smaller sizes to gather and frame in groups to create your own art gallery. If you want to reproduce the beauty of **pencil renderings**, use a copy machine to print copyright-free line art onto rag stock paper that is hand fed into the machine. The texture of the paper will reproduce the accented pencil lines of the original art and easily pass for the real thing. Frame them to complete the authentic-looking replicas.

FLORA

Don't forget **plants** as a decoration. Large plants add life to the room by introducing a natural element. They create a more peaceful environment and can evoke feelings of everything from a small garden to a tropical jungle. Of course, **flowers** are also noted for their attention-getting appeal. Whether you use single stems in a collection of bud vases or large bouquets to fill the room with a pleasant, floral aroma, no faux chic living room would be complete without bringing a bit of the outdoors inside.

Collectibles

Collectibles typically provide emotional substance because they are usually collected with passion. They can be sentimental in nature—perhaps mementos from a family vacation. They can be small or large in scale—a set of silver sugar spoons, a series of porcelain figurines, or a pair of statues retrieved from a relative's attic. Overall, these "must have" items contextualize a life, one item at a time.

DECORATIVE GLASS

Decorative glass has a special appeal to many home decorators. It is the collectible that makes its appearance in a play of light and transparent color. Situate glass pieces together with votive candles. Cut-crystal **vases**, engraved **stemware**, and even vintage **bottles** and jelly **jars** can attract the eye as light sparkles through their refracting surfaces. Line up your collections across your mantel, on side tables, or on your coffee table to spark conversation while entertaining or to simply gaze upon while enjoying some solitude.

URNS

Classical styling with an air of Greek history, large garden urns tend to have a masculine feel that goes well with minimalist style, and they can be displayed both indoors and out. What's more, they look beautiful whether they are on their own or filled with silk or real flowers. Surprisingly, decorative urns need not be made of metal. Plastic and plaster urns can be painted or patinated to resemble metal or stone. Peruse your local craft or hobby store for spray-painting kits in metal and stone finishes for the quickest and easiest route to the result you want.

STATUARY

Statuary always introduces drama in a decorating scheme. Collect miniature busts of famous composers or single out favorite Greek gods, lining them up on majestic columns. Even a solitary bust of a goddess can be a compelling presence in a room, as seen on page 63.

The Kitchen

HISTORICALLY, THE KITCHEN WAS A ROOM OF EARNEST, SIMPLE FUNCTION, WHERE FOOD was stored and meals were prepared. Because the room was typically off-limits to guests, a woman, who usually ruled the space, was able to keep hidden the secrets of her culinary magic and the mess. Unfortunately, too etiquette-bound to invite visitors into the kitchen, her forays out to the dining room were clipped into momentary parcels so she wouldn't jeopardize whatever it was that was bubbling on the stove.

Over the years, the kitchen has evolved into one of the busiest rooms in the house. No longer a purely functional space, the kitchen has become "life central"—the room where family and friends alike flock for conversation, while scrumptious stew is coming off the stove and just-baked bread is coming out of the oven, and where the chef and the guests can join in the camaraderie of food preparation. Guests are now free to enjoy a glass of wine with the hostess as she cooks and to do the chopping, dicing, stirring, and tasting, as the sharing unfolds.

Thankfully, entertaining is no longer relegated to the dining room—all can be accomplished right in the kitchen if one is so inclined. With this social evolution, the utilitarian agenda that once defined the kitchen's strict rules and practical simplicity grew to reflect a home space with life and personality, an evolution that has naturally evolved to include the way the kitchen looks, with a keen eye to integrating the aesthetics and the everyday functions required of the space. Certainly, the underlying purpose of any efficient kitchen remains its *raison d'etre*, and you keep it in mind whether you decorate with the sleek, modern lines of brushed-steel appliances or with the reassuring shapes of white enamel stoves and hand-held eggbeaters, as long as your kitchen serves and comforts you.

OPPOSITE

The softly gathered panels of a sturdy cotton fabric sport a fresh windowpane plaid in muted apple green and butter yellow in this cozy kitchen. The panels decorate the lower counters, hiding the sink's plumbing. Reassuringly retro, the skirted decoration frames the narrow counter made of wooden boards that offer a practical surface for cutting, chopping, and letting dishes drip dry. A flowerpot filled with a little boxwood plant is cleverly wrapped with paper and tied with twine. The farmhouse-style ladder-back chair is painted white, with visible wear-and-tear on the edges of the slat back; it sits behind a simple pine table, left bare of any obvious finish or ornamentation except for a floral tablecloth with a wide green border laid neatly in place.

Strictly speaking, every kitchen requires basic appliances and some furniture, however minimal—a table and chairs and, what you may symbolically refer to as "furniture," the cabinetry and storage spaces. Although this list is rather basic, it is the foundation on which you instinctively plan and build your stylistic environment, expressing your sensibilities through your choice of color, pattern, and texture. If you inherit old kitchen counters, you know immediately if you like them or not, and on some deep level, you move to accept them or change them. You do the same with the appliances, those behemoths that demand attention by virtue of their function and size. Decoration in the kitchen may have been a frivolous afterthought at one time, but it is now a natural part of how you approach the space, down to the drawer pulls and cupboard knobs. In what other room are the fundamental goals of nourishment and personal connection so linked? It is the kitchen that calls to mind some of your strongest memories: a room infused with the aroma of just-brewed coffee or soup simmering on the stove, and the sound of lingering conversations shared around tables and countertops, interrupted only by laughter or the clank of cutlery against china. The kitchen epitomizes hearth and home, and no corner should remain untouched as you seek to personalize it and work within it.

 General information on selected faux effects has been provided and is noted with this icon. However, be sure to consult "Sources and Resources" on pages 139 to 141 for more detailed information that will help ensure professional-looking results and provide important working safeguards.

Faux Effects for Architectural Elements

WALLS

Many kitchens do not have the vast, bare wall space that, say, a dining room does, mainly because of the obligatory cabinetry, shelving, and appliances that typically occupy and break up the line and surface of much of the space. But, do not think for one moment that this limitation diminishes the possibilities that are available to you when you set out to create the faux chic kitchen you desire.

Prepping Your Walls for Painting

Before you paint, it is important to prepare your walls.

- Repair any cracks or holes using spackle, to ensure a smooth, flat surface.

- Remove all grease and grime that has accumulated on your walls, because these substances will prevent paint from adhering evenly.

- It is best to prime your walls before you paint, particularly if the walls are a dark color. The primer paint will reduce the ghosting effects from the dark pigments already on the wall, especially if you are applying a lighter paint color over it.

- Use paint finishes in satin and semigloss to give your walls an attractive if slight sheen that will reflect light beautifully and protect against the natural aftereffects of cooking.

FAUX PAINT EFFECTS

A simple coat of paint may be all you need to brighten your kitchen and help you see it in a new way. Although any paint effect mentioned in *Faux Chic* can be used in your kitchen, the photographs that follow will provide you with some traditional and nontraditional examples of wall treatments that will inspire your chic self, regardless of where you apply them.

ABOVE

The graphic fluency of this fantastic kitchen is illustrated in the bold color and line that sweep over the soft green walls, decorated in brush strokes that configure into oversized vines, leaves, flowers, and vegetables. These large, abstract botanical motifs were painted freehand, creating striking accents and shifting focal points that lead the eye to the second application of this same design idea, this time continued on a smaller scale on a narrow wall shelf, the cabinet fronts, and the tall stools. Adding to the visual interest are the check and plaid patterns of the soft furnishings and accessories.

If painting a kitchen wall a solid color is too mundane for your taste, there are a number of ways to add spice to plain color. The kitchen featured on page 69 illustrates the dynamic interest **line art** can add to walls painted a single background color. The two-stage process of creating this look is straightforward. First, the walls were painted a soft green color, which could stand on its own. Yet, with a little added creativity, the freehand spontaneity of strokes from an artist's paintbrush turned these soft green walls into a canvas filled with imagination and beauty. Granted, there is talent and experience revealed in the drawing and the overall work, but with today's sources for decorative **stencils**, similar designs can be applied successfully by any home decorator.

The **faux stone** look on walls is so beautiful, you may want to create the same effect on your floors. The basic technical principles apply. In addition, you may also want to experiment with different shapes and use different color paints to recreate the look of marble, granite, and terra-cotta tile, all decorative stones that are arranged in block configurations. The challenge is to study the gradations of color and pattern in each material and render convincing copies. Marble and granite are the most difficult to reproduce, requiring painting experience, whereas tile is the easiest to reproduce.

OPPOSITE

A graceful metal pitcher arrests the eye and calls attention to a stone block wall in this appealing kitchen. On closer inspection, the stone blocks reveal themselves to be painted on, a convincing faux effect created with tape and paint. Lending an air of antiquity, the restrained use of the faux finish confers classical elegance to an otherwise up-to-date domain, where modern appliances and new wood counters do not break the spell set by the stone wall. A decorative clay jug perched on a shelf carries the stylistic message of Mesopotamia. An open cupboard attached to the wall appears to have been commandeered from a larger armoire, called into service as the keeper of an eclectic collection of unique accessories—a Staffordshire dog, porcelain plates and vases, and a glazed earthenware bowl and pitcher.

Creating Faux Stone

For another faux look, consider treating your walls to a faux stone effect.

- Lay down strips of tape in a configuration of a wall of stone blocks. The tape masks off and simultaneously creates the mortar lines between the blocks of stone. Remember that the ground color on the wall determines the color of the faux mortar. The open, nonmasked areas define the stone blocks themselves.

- After the tape is laid out in a grid pattern, use a sponge or rag to blot on thin layers of color.

To recreate the look of the grainy surface of stone, examine actual samples for information about texture and color. The colorwashing technique naturally creates the desired layering and shifting density of color associated with real stone. Another way to enhance the faux illusion is to add sand to the paint. Available in grades from fine to coarse, sand becomes trapped by the paint and adheres to the wall, creating a rough texture. If you mix the sand and paint yourself, test it out on a section of wall to see how it behaves. Ultimately, you can skip the whole paint-and-sand mixing process by buying commercially available preparations.

Commonly found in the kitchen, **tiles** are available in a vast assortment of colors, styles, and sizes, offering endless possibilities for your chic decor. Although you may have entire walls paved in tiles in your bathroom, it is more common to find tiles applied in smaller areas in the kitchen—for example, on the backsplash by the sink. Whatever look you desire, keep in mind that ceramic tiles are heavy and need strong adhesive to install properly. Installing real tiles requires some experience, so you may want to consult an expert before starting a job.

If you have existing tiles and wish to add painted decoration, you can. What's more, you can completely change the color of your kitchen tiles using ceramic and glass paint, or you can simply change the style of the tile by adding little details, like florets and geometric motifs. For example, you can freehand paint a small fleur-de-lis on each tile, or inscribe words like *basil* and *thyme* for a kitchen wall arrangement. Stenciling is another option for adding decorative accents with ease. In the kitchen featured on page 86, a tea-party theme featuring stenciled cups, saucers, and teapots is presented in French blue on glossy white tile. It is also important to note that it is not necessary to keep your images within the confines of one tile. As seen with the teapots, strong impact is made by their size, their contours overflowing into adjacent areas measuring three or four tiles high, and one or two tiles wide.

FAUX TEXTURAL EFFECTS

Whether your intention is to create a textural effect on all your kitchen walls or just a portion of one, the techniques illustrated below can help you achieve the look you want.

Colorwashing is an easy technique, described in more detail on page 18. Essentially, it uses washes of color over plaster walls to create a welcoming room with a Mediterranean feel. In what could have remained an ordinary room, a kitchen with plain white walls has been transformed summarily through the use of texture and color. As seen in the kitchen on page 74, plaster walls—the texture of which has been manipulated while wet—are suddenly brought to life when color is introduced. A soft blue has been colorwashed onto the lower portion of the wall, creating a band of arresting color that draws the eye to an inset shelf and to the plump pillows on a painted bench. The ceiling that once held dark wood beams is now showcased, painted in the same blue as the wall and door frame. The band of applied wall color and the ceiling architecture both defines and lowers the perceived height of the room.

Creating Faux Tiles

You can use paint to reproduce the look of tiles, without spending a lot of time or money. The technique is similar to the one used to create stone block:

- First, mask off the tiles on the wall using tape, making the squares any size you like. Faux multicolored tiles in smaller sizes can add a bit of whimsy to your kitchen, whereas larger tiles may conjure the elegance of European palaces.

- Then, paint the faux tiles.

- To make them more authentic looking, add sand to the paint for added texture, and after applying the paint, use a rag to rub off some pigment in the center of the tiles for the handcrafted appearance of kiln-baked tiles, like the ones on the opposite page. Another option is to apply multilayers of high-gloss paint to the faux tile, to achieve the shine and depth associated with some glazed ceramic tiles.

Framed glass doors protect the china and glassware in a pair of kitchen cabinets separated by a four-pane window structurally underlined by a narrow glass shelf. This is the perfect site for a collection of colored glass and china—a mouth-blown cup, molded bottles and pitchers, a jar of sea glass, egg cups in latticework designs, and a stout teapot with a pewter lid. Below the shelf is a configuration of glazed tiles in a random arrangement of blue, ochre, moss green, and rust. A backsplash of faux tiles can be reproduced using tape and paint.

You can also create interesting texture and designs on your kitchen walls using mosaic tiles or other materials arranged in a mosaic-style pattern. **Mosaic tiles** are available in craft stores and come in various colors and sizes. With the right tools, you can easily break them into less conventional shapes. Mosaic tiles are available in glass, ceramic, and resins, each material offering its own distinct design characteristics that affect the artistic feel of the finished design. The idea of a mosaic design is to arrange small chips of colored tile in a way that forms a picture or a pattern. The grand baths in ancient Rome used mosaic tiles as decoration, plotting out intricately rendered portraits of deities using $1/2$-inch squares.

Mosaic tilework need not be relegated to simple square patterns or small kitchen spaces. If you have time and patience, you can craft truly **original tile art** in your kitchen as seen on this page. Mosaics can be created from household items, such as broken china plates and teacups, their painted designs lending to the overall mosaic. Ordinary items like buttons, beads, shells, and small mirrors can also be used, depending on the look you want. To affix the mosaic pieces, use epoxy, grout, or cement. The spaces between the pieces can be filled in with the same material or with one that takes color. Tinting grout, for example, provides the option to create harmony with the prevailing colorway of the tiles, thereby reducing the sense of chunks of color. Or grout may be tinted in sharp contrast, revealing the parts that went into forming the mosaic pattern. Remember that adhering the tiles to the wall or other substratum is important, so consult other references to avoid costly problems. Remember, too, that tiles—even smaller, mosaic-style ones—add weight to the tiled surface.

ABOVE

What may have started as an ornate backsplash confined to the area behind this petite sink might have inspired such creativity that the artisan expanded the mosaic to include a framed mirror and the entire face of a cabinet. Using a combination of faceted stones that appear commercially broken and shards of colored glass in various shades of blue, the coloration of the mosaic design works in conjunction with the wall colorwashed a sky blue.

OPPOSITE

A Mediterranean sensibility fills the air in the eating area of this open kitchen. Ceiling beams are painted the color of pale lapis lazuli, as is the door frame, curtained off by a swath of gauzy white cotton. Echoing the blue and white colorway are the plaster walls, colorwashed into two distinct sections—the top two-thirds painted a broad, horizontal band of stark white and the bottom strip of plaster painted a pale blue. The surface of the colorwashed plaster has degraded into large blisters of paint, unavoidable effects of the humidity and changing seaside temperatures. Furnished with a distressed trestle table, a painted bench, and side table, the cavernous armoire across the tile floor is painted white, completing the welcoming chic feel.

FLOORS

COVERED FLOORS

The floor in your kitchen provides yet another canvas on which to express your creativity and your faux chic style. Whether you want to add a few **area rugs**, throw down a hand-painted **floor cloth** you fashioned yourself, or **paint** an elaborate geometric pattern directly on the floor, your decision can affect the total look of your kitchen. Whether your floor is made of wood, stone, brick, or some other material, you can accent it with decorative coverings that coordinate with the other furnishings. Whatever you choose, keep in mind that because the kitchen is one of the busiest rooms in your home, it is important to keep your floors and coverings in good condition. After you determine the high-traffic areas, you can make a sound choice for situating rugs and for maintaining the condition of the floors themselves.

OPPOSITE

In this kitchen, the distinctive plaid design of a Burberry scarf doubles as a curtain and dictates the prevailing pattern for the walls painted to mimic wallpaper. Decorated in an oversized version of the Burberry plaid, the wall pattern is rendered in the signature camel, black, white, and red colorway, neatly painted using a masking tape method. The faux plaid wallpaper is a witty foil for the oak cabinets and drawers painted black, the brushed steel dishwasher, and the striped pattern on the floor, a simpler version of the plaid pattern. An upper cupboard is painted red inside, continuing the colorful dialogue begun by the fringed scarf hung like a valance on the window.

Creating Faux Plaid Wallpaper

To recreate the Burberry pattern on your wall, use an actual Burberry item as a guide.

- Apply a base coat of camel-colored paint.

- When the paint is dry, use a chalk line to mark off the Burberry pattern line-for-line, or conjure a design of your own. You may want to work with a partner to ensure straight and perpendicular lines on your walls.

- Then, mark off the red stripes using parallel strips of tape spaced an inch or two apart, depending on the desired thickness of the stripe. Follow the pattern marked in pencil as a guide. Use a paint roller to apply the red paint between the strips.

- Follow that with a swipe of a sawtooth scraper, to replicate the striations shown in the photograph.

- When the painted stripes are dry, add the vertical black and the white stripes, using the same method described above.

- Repeat the process, laying down the horizontal black and then the white stripes.

You can carry the design to the floor, expressing a simplified version, using the masking technique; on the opposite page, only vertical stripes in black, white, and red are applied over the camel-colored base coat. Be sure the paint on the floor is completely dry before you apply two or three coats of sealer to preserve all your hard work.

PAINTED FLOORS

Painting a floor is an easy way to hide significant wear and tear, cover an undesirable material, or take advantage of the perfect "canvas" underfoot. Regardless of your motivation, painting your kitchen floor a **solid color** that coordinates with the other design elements provides a convenient way to tie all the decorative elements together. Even light-colored floors painted in a soft cream or milky white can transport you to the Vermont farmhouse with the well-worn floors where you played as a child. This look and the feelings it evokes can be brought home to your very own kitchen to enjoy. If you decide to paint your floor, do not limit yourself to pale washes of color. Buttercup yellow, fire engine red, or cobalt blue can make a fabulous impression. It all depends on what best expresses your fantasy chic kitchen.

If you do want to add a little something to liven up a floor that is painted a solid color, add a large **central motif**—for example, fun, geometric shapes pooled in the center of the room or under the kitchen table, as shown in the photograph on the opposite page. Here, a graphic-style medallion comprises a large red star painted within a black circle surrounded by a yellow diamond outlined in red. When the medallion is viewed in relation to the large field of deep green in which it is situated, it stands out. The medallion is slightly smaller than the round table and chairs that surround it, and it forms a practical design element-cum-faux carpet to the seating area, without being in danger of being scuffed off by the chair legs. All the shapes that were drawn and painted are simple to do. You can map out the design using masking tape. If these shapes do not appeal to you, by all means experiment with other combinations, borrowing the geometrically strong hexagonal signs painted on Pennsylvania barns. Or, stencil floral motifs in select places to accent the painted floor, or shells and boats to accent the floor of a beach house.

ABOVE

The warmth of the Van Gogh yellow is limewashed over the plaster walls in this rustic kitchen. The saturated wall color brightens the room and is further enhanced by the ambient light coming though mullioned French doors situated at the far end of the room, outside the frame of the picture. A collection of tin boxes is lined up on the mantel of the large stone fireplace, an early site of cauldrons and roasts turning on spits, where now sits a delicate table laid with a child's enamelware tea set. A nearby wood table and five chairs show the warm patina of surfaces touched throughout the years. A stack of French stoneware plates with fancy detailing are wheel thrown and glazed in vitreous ochre, a signature color of decorators in the southern France.

OPPOSITE

The entry wall serves as a decorative prelude to this cheerful kitchen. Pears and apples are stenciled onto the wall with acrylic paint. The adjacent door frame is painted white and leads to a sun-filled room furnished with a round table in polished maple and a quartet of sturdy office chairs painted hunter green. The painted floor beneath the table is emblazoned with a hand-painted diamond-and-star medallion, its yellow field coordinating with the furnishings situated at the back wall—a plate rack and a low dresser both painted banana yellow to match the walls.

Lighting

Most kitchens receive sufficient natural light during the day to fulfill their designated functions; however, with little exception, kitchens require some kind of artificial light in the evening when darkness descends outside. Because the kitchen continues to function at full throttle, often into the wee hours, ensuring adequate **spot lighting** around work areas and cooking spaces not only is important but also requires planning. Lighting certainly plays an important role when the kitchen table functions as a desk space for paying bills, doing homework, or laying out craft projects, so planning for these uses is important, too.

When you look through the illustrations in this chapter, examine the ways in which lighting is used. Various types of **hanging lamps** are pictured throughout: one with a crenellated glass **shade** on page 78, one with a bouquet of industrial-looking bulbs on joints on page 69, one with a linen table napkin draped over the shade on page 79, one with an antique **lantern** converted to electricity, and one with a hoop of filigree suspended from hooks with **wrought-iron** flowers and holders for candles on page 74.

Besides being essential to illuminating our tabletop activities, lighting also serves an important emotional function. Rarely do the long bulbs of yesterday's neon lights answer the call for light that embraces the spirit. More commonly, mood is simultaneously created and supported by modulating the intensity of incandescent light, its yellow cast warming up colors with the flick of a switch. Soft lighting can also be provided with **candles**, evidenced by the popular use of votive candles housed in cut-crystal glasses, tall tapered candles, and cathedral-sized pillar candles.

Lighting can help to support the stylistic direction you have taken in your kitchen, casting interesting shadows and revealing the contours of your furnishings—or camouflaging the imperfect surfaces on floors and walls. Lighting can also spotlight favorite things, like collectibles, and it is especially useful in spotlighting your artistic efforts. If you have painstakingly applied a faux finish to a wall, illuminate your work with small lamps. If you have applied a particularly handsome decorative pattern to the floor, show it off using **overhead lighting** or spot lighting.

In your commitment to transforming what were the strictly functional spaces in your kitchen into zones that are cozy and beautiful, you will find yourself turning to lighting to set the intimate moods that lead you back to the kitchen for tea at midnight when the overstuffed couch in the den might be a more logical choice. The gravitational pull of the kitchen is based on the perceptual shift that occurs when you treat the kitchen to the same careful attention to detail that you do other rooms. After all, it is these details that make the room yours.

OPPOSITE

This near-cartoon mix of graphic patterns, colors, and patinas animates this modern kitchen with a retro feel. A hip place to sip mint juleps and rendezvous with an exotic stranger, the round metal cafe table is set for two. The brushed stainless-steel cabinetry and appliances reflect the checkerboard floor, blocked out in white and rich brown tiles. Molded chairs with spindly chrome legs are made from lime green and aquamarine polystyrene. Despite its sleek lines and cool modernity, the room is neither austere nor sterile. There is a palpable romance in the scattered vases holding single blooms, in the fuchsia lampshade glowing like a distant planet, and in the votive candles resting on the framed oven hood and the refrigerator— flames flickering like summer lightning bugs.

ABOVE

An antique grain bin that now serves as counter space dominates this
century-old kitchen, which fortunately has been minimally updated, leaving
its architectural and aesthetic integrity solidly intact. Besides the gleam
of a modern stove with a sleek overhead hood and lighting fixtures, the
natural colors of sun and soil play over the provincial space, expressed in
a hutch hand painted in a folk style à la Carib, a backsplash paved with
chipped local stones and shards of colored glass, and a floor laid with
kiln-fired tiles. Mismatched wooden chairs are decorated with unique
geometric patterns and primitive markings reminiscent of tribal art. They
surround a skillfully painted faux marble table.

Furniture

Some of the best daily rituals begin at the kitchen table, like having a cup of hot coffee in the morning, reading the newspaper, or spending time with children before they rush off to school. The furniture in the kitchen must support the needs of the family, which dictate that it be practical and sturdy, as well as stylish and imaginative.

Kitchen furniture, like the dining room furniture, can include anything that allows your family and guests to move safely and comfortably within the space, while fulfilling the culinary ministrations of eating or entertaining. Whether your kitchen needs a large wooden **table** with matching **chairs** or a small middle **island** with a few **barstools**, only a few pieces are actually essential to serving you and making your kitchen function.

The kitchen is a great domain in which you can create one-of-a-kind pieces from common finds, such as the recycled grain bin on the opposite page. The low dresser featured on page 78 can be transformed into a farmhouse-chic chest by adding a crackle finish. It could also be turned into a French chest by adding carved details and fancy hardware, and loading its top with fancy collectibles. Search flea markets and thrift stores for tables and chairs with interesting shapes, making sure they are structurally sound. Even mismatched chairs look great together when united by an organizing design principle such as color. Look for drawer pulls and knobs, escutcheons, and switch plates in home-decorating stores that sell vintage reproductions. Even the most ordinary cabinet can benefit from this easy face-lift approach.

BELOW

A profusion of flowering plants collects in a dry sink, cascading toward the plain wood cabinets below, each front panel featuring a scene from Aesop's fables, each scene depicted in delicately drawn illustrations painted on a cream background. On one panel, a crow facing a jug is framed by the interwoven stems of a rosebush, each leafy branch accented with pink blooms; on the next panel, a fox turns toward a lacy grapevine shaped like an inverted L; on the last panel, the fox looks up at the crow, who is now perched high above him on a leafy branch. Although freehand painting was used to decorate these cabinet doors, stencils can also be used to map out the basic shapes, with freehand details added afterward.

LEFT

The rustic elements of this country kitchen are stylistically homogenized with creamy white paint—from the sloping ceiling to the wide plank walls decorated with a row of architectural rosettes retrieved from demolition, to the recycled cabinet fronts decorated with open frames made from cut branches, to the plate rack above the sink. The tranquility of the all-cream domain is interrupted by hits of strong color—the red apples on enamelware bowls, a cardinal red pillow, and the red-and-black checkerboard on a chipped and peeling game table.

Even if your kitchen has modern **appliances**, it does not necessarily have to carry the modern look throughout. As seen in the kitchen on page 71, the shiny stainless steel stove is offset by wood cabinets painted a soft green, stone walls done in shades of cream and beige, and ancient-looking urns and paintings that give the kitchen an overall classic appearance, without sacrificing the necessary modern conveniences.

Because cabinetry can occupy the majority of space in a small kitchen or a significant amount of usable space in a larger one, it is best to treat cabinets as one conceptual unit, integrating them into a homogenous whole using color, pattern, or surface textures. The most straightforward approach to **cabinetry** is to preserve it in its original state, assuming the wood has a pleasing finish and is in good

Adding Woodwork to Plain Cabinets

Another way to spruce up cabinets, as illustrated on the opposite page, is to add woodwork to them:

- First, apply a coat of creamy white paint to all cabinet surfaces.

- Then measure and miter the ends of straight branches configured into frames to fit your cabinet fronts. Be aware that the woodworking process to create these frames is tedious, and experience is necessary to accurately and safely cut the needed branches. If you prefer, consult a local lumberyard for help. You may be able to have an expert cut the mitered ends of the branches for a nominal fee.

- Mark a custom-fit rectangle or square on each cabinet front. Use it as a guide to position, glue, and nail the pieces in place, butting the mitered ends neatly together.

- Paint the cabinets overall, as shown.

Ragging, Sponging, and Staining

Whether you decide to rag, sponge, or stain your walls, the technique you choose will invariably add its own distinct color, texture, and grain to the surface. Although all of the techniques are relatively simple, the methods do vary.

RAGGING OR SPONGING

- Clean the cabinets, removing any accumulated dirt and grime. Also remove the hardware.

- Paint the cabinet the desired color.

- Then, use a rag or sponge to lift off some of the paint to create visual texture.

STAINING

- Clean the cabinets, removing any accumulated dirt and grime. Also remove the hardware.

- Apply a colorwash or tinted wood stain to raw wood.

- Then, apply several protective coats of varnish to create a subtle veil of color and a visible grain.

condition, that the age and style of the cabinets appeal to you, and, less important, that the cabinets harmonize with rest of the kitchen decor. If the cabinets are hardwood, consider a coat of wax and a good buffing before applying the difficult-to-correct paint job that can cover up a beautiful wood grain. If, by contrast, the cabinets are veneered particleboard or are falling apart, go ahead and transform them using faux effects.

FAUX PAINT EFFECTS

Colorwashing, ragging, sponging, and staining each creates a distinct and interesting effect when applied to wood. Be sure to examine the furniture sections in the other chapters to develop a broader understanding of the scope and range of these faux effects. These same technical principles can be applied to wood cabinetry. Understand, too, that

ABOVE

An assortment of shapely woven baskets hangs from the exposed beams in this bright kitchen. The baskets are within easy reach for use during trips to the garden, where they are filled with just-picked summer flowers and voluptuous tomatoes warm from the sun. Some larger baskets hold flowers that have been allowed to dry in situ, and a couple of tin lanterns have been tucked between them. On the far wall, a high shelf holds several porcelain mantel clocks, their unmoving hands indicating the precise time they stopped ticking. On a lower shelf in the same open cupboard sit two wobbly towers of nesting porcelain cups and a little collection of hot chocolate pots. Lovely illustrations of porcelain jars, pots, and dishes are stenciled delft-style on the wall tiles, shifting your perception to the prevailing blue-and-white coloration of the china crowding the shelves' remaining spaces.

OPPOSITE

The top of this antique pine hutch holds a collection of vintage food packages, evoking a remembered walk down the aisles of a supermarket in 1950s America. The hutch has two hardworking sections: a top china cupboard enclosed by a pair of eight-pane doors, and a closed stout cupboard on the bottom section with crudely made recessed panel doors. Its waist-high work surface is topped surprisingly with a decorative slab of green stone, perhaps a practical recent addition. What is evident in the soft, honey tones of the aged wood and the honesty of its structural lines is the value of preserving the original finish of old pieces. This one testifies to that end.

your personality will naturally affect your efforts, adding unique characteristics and style to all that you do. Check your local craft store and library for graphic materials if you need inspiration for faux finishes.

A **freehand design** like the one on the hutch on page 69 can also be seen on the painted cabinet fronts. The artisan-made checkerboards, stars, swirls, and dots all come alive, adding energy and movement to the space. Although the designs were rendered freehand, a similar effect can be accomplished using **rubber stamps**. Available in every imaginable theme, from geometric to floral motifs, rubber stamps can be used to print line drawings directly onto sealed wood; follow with a coat of protective varnish.

Collectibles

For many, kitchen collectibles include the tools and vessels needed and used for cooking. Although their instant accessibility may dictate your first impulse to display them, their functional aesthetic is typically what engages interest and sends collectors into stores looking for just the right racks, shelves, and hooks on which to display them. For the most part, however, romance with kitchen vessels is usually inspired by the character and color of the materials from which the **vessels** are made. Perhaps you enjoy looking at the peach-orange glow of a row of copper pots and feeling the heft of one in your hands, or you appreciate the utility of stainless steel **tools,** like long-handled forks and spoons, seemingly made for a giant's table. Without a doubt, these collectibles capture the imaginations and incite reflection. Items that resonate on a deeper level—for example, items that pull you back to your childhood or to your family's country of origin—are also common collectibles, even though they may serve no other function. You may collect every **basket** you can, use only a few, and still find room for the many more you may never use, as seen on page 86. A flash of memory of making baked

goods with a favorite aunt may send you out looking for the same hand-operated eggbeater just to recapture the essence of that time—and you may come home happy, not because you found the illusive contraption but because you found another "must have," perhaps a **canister set** of boxy cubes with lids made in glazed stoneware that have *sucre, farine,* and *cafe* printed in capital letters, as seen on page 86.

The creative impulses that drive you to collect one kind of precious thing instead of another may be rooted in the colors or patterns of the vintage curtains you pick up at a flea market, or they may be connected to a special occasion, such as when your firstborn was wrapped in a Provençal *boutis,* or harken back to the chandelier that lit your first home. Often, the right collectible turns up—the little lamp with a beaded shade that matches one you already have, the carved fish made in New England that completes a collection (as seen on page 87), an old manual typewriter with keys that work—and suddenly the indefinable is defined, revealed in the stirrings of the heart.

RIGHT

The symphony of "life enjoyed to the fullest" is manifest in every detail in this large Provençal kitchen. Beginning with the notes struck by the personal collection of antique plates, platters, jars, and bowls that line the fireplace undermantel, echoing the blue-and-white designs found on the tile hearth. More gorgeous plates and jugs politely crowd the overmantel, where a pair of gilt candelabra add regal presence to the careful arrangement. A lantern-style chandelier picks up the aristocratic melody and expresses it in its intricately cast arms with delicate leaf and beading details, each candle cup ending in a candle. Earthenware jugs and a glass vase are filled with a profusion of flowers, some in monochromatic bouquets of fuchsia and yellow. What is stunningly clear in this kitchen is its lived-in feel. Despite the museum-quality antiques that fill the room, especially the round fruitwood table and cane-back carved chairs, this life-affirming domain is filled with life-affirming presence of family.

The Bedroom

THE BEDROOM IS TYPICALLY THE MOST PRIVATE ROOM IN ANY HOME. IT IS THE ROOM in which people are the most vulnerable, the room in which they need to feel the most cosseted and the most personally grounded. Even though a simple cot might suffice to ensure the requisite good night's sleep, the bedroom also serves to support the more spiritual needs for calm and comfort. Whether you lay out handmade quilts replete with tatters or enclose plump pillows with care-intensive, intricately embroidered linen, you do it because you instinctively understand what it takes to make you comfortable. It is this faithfulness to self that is at the true heart of chic. As you move through the decorating ideas in the featured bedrooms, you will be inspired to treat your own space to the faux effects shown.

General information on selected faux effects has been provided and is noted with this icon. However, be sure to consult "Sources and Resources" on pages 139 to 141 for more detailed information that will help ensure professional-looking results and provide important working safeguards.

Faux Effects for Architectural Elements

WALLS

What first conveys the feeling of the bedroom is the color of the walls. Although it bears repeating that your faux chic sensibilities should determine your ultimate choice of color, a simple metaphor may be helpful. Think of color in the bedroom as a tone of voice: soft colors, especially pastels, are like calming whispers or words spoken in low tones; by contrast, bright primary colors and bold patterns are shouts for attention. Your felt sense, of course, will determine your choice, radiating your interpretation of intimacy and style.

FAUX PAINT EFFECTS

Little compares to the exultant joy in creating the look of striped wallpaper. Paint and masking tape are the secrets to successfully and easily adding stripes to your walls. Essentially, the **faux striped wallpaper** look is based on a technique of applying wide masking tape at even, parallel intervals to a flat wall. The strips of tape conceal the wall's background color. When a second color of paint is applied over the spaces and the tape is removed, a two-color striped pattern is revealed.

Choosing **colors that surprise and awaken** can be especially liberating in a room like the bedroom, noted for its muted sensibilities. On page 90, a bedroom wall is painted in a stripe pattern in red and gold. The stripes set up a daring backdrop for the more traditional elements placed in this faux chic bedroom.

If you prefer to use more tangible references when making your color choice, take your cues from the natural world to see what shades go well together. Study the subtle hues on a seashell, for example. Or, look at a country landscape at dawn for a range of color ideas. Your inspiration will come from everywhere, and you will know immediately what works for you. If you prefer, do a test patch of painted color on a remote part of your bedroom wall, allowing natural light to inform the overall effect; then, check out the coloration under artificial light. In this way, you can evaluate the color before painting the walls.

Overall, the value of using **colorwashing**, especially in the bedroom, is that you can visually assess the changing tones of color as you go along, adding more glaze or even a different tint of glaze until you have achieved the drama or calm you desire. For example, the bedroom on the opposite page illustrates the colorwashing technique. Using a light blue ground color with a subtle hint of pink, the colorwashed layers in a soft shade of ultramarine blue glaze are applied with a brush and a rag, resulting in the

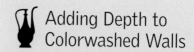

Adding Depth to Colorwashed Walls

One of the easiest ways to add color while still maintaining the tranquillity of the bedroom is to use the colorwash approach when applying color to your walls. Colorwashing is a process of applying several coats of tinted glaze over a ground color. With each successive application of glaze, a richer and, in some cases, more intense, color is achieved. You can add even more dynamic depth to a color-washed wall by **dry brushing** or **ragging** the still-wet tint, creating a distressed look. In another approach, you can take down the color to some degree after the tinted glaze dries thoroughly, using a fine- to medium-grade sandpaper. By **rubbing** over the paint, underlayers of color are revealed in soft patchy veils. The soft tonal quality of this treatment is reminiscent of the ancient frescoes common to medieval churches and palaces.

shifting tonalities and dimension of azure skies. Although blue tends to be a cooler color, it can be warmed up slightly by first applying a warm white to the walls as a ground color. Or, you can begin with soft peachy shades, adding white as a second glaze coat.

OPPOSITE

The ethereal calm of this French-styled bedroom is established in the color-washed walls subtly distressed in shifting tones of blue using a dry brush and rag on the still-wet glaze. The carved chair is upholstered in a cheeky plaid fabric, and the window drape sports a bold awning stripe. A tile floor in a honeycomb pattern leads to the curvaceous lines of an antique dresser, painted blue and picked out in gold leaf. The French carved frame of the gilded mirror reflects the gossamer swaths of cotton hung from the top rails of a painted iron bed.

FAUX TEXTURAL EFFECTS

The effect of finishing an ordinary wall made of sheet rock so that its surface resembles plaster is surprisingly easy. The way to achieve the look of **faux plaster** is discussed on page 48. Its distinctive look adds texture to the wall and imbues the room with exotic cultural cues that speak of Morocco, Greece, and Italy. It is no wonder that the effect is used so often. Although it is tempting to leave the chalky white color of the raw plaster "as is," it is also appealing to exploit plaster's inherent properties—that of porosity and surface "hand"—to add color and pattern.

Tinting plaster adds veils of color. A subtle tint can be applied to the entire wall for an overall mottled color as shown in the attic bedroom on page 98 where sunlight plays patterns over the walls painted apple green; it can also be used selectively on particular areas of the wall to establish a graphic pattern as featured in the bedroom suite on the opposite page. In this bedroom, the pairing of solid tinting and a patterned tinting treatment is illustrated. A blue-and-white stripe pattern lives peacefully with a wall tinted overall in the same blue.

OPPOSITE

Natural light floods this Mediterranean bedroom where bold sweeps of blue and red set up dramatic tension. A grand doorway arch, delineated in painted woodwork, separates the dressing area from the boudoir spaces joined by a tile floor. On the far plaster wall, wide stripes are roughed out in blue using a tinting technique, and a graphic blue-and-white check fabric is hung nonchalantly in the armoire, adding witty counterpoint. A French *boutis* in rich red covers the round table and calls attention to the bed, dressed in a red blanket and white linen and draped in a blue bed curtain.

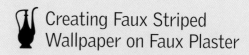

Creating Faux Striped Wallpaper on Faux Plaster

- Make sure the room is well ventilated.

- Then, run lengths of masking tape set approximately a foot apart on the faux plaster wall you wish to treat. The tape will define the surface area of the stripe. Technically, it is important to understand that the tape will not inhibit the tint from bleeding past the designated line of the tape. To ensure a basically clean stripe, apply the tint between the bands of tape, leaving a margin next to the side of the tape on either side to accommodate the natural bleeding action of the tint.

- Apply a thin wash of alkali-resistant tint first, but do not overload your brush. (It is important that the tint be alkali-resistant so that the pigment does not completely fade.) The tint may run, depending upon its consistency. You can always add more tint to strengthen the intensity of the color.

- When the tint has dried, remove the tape.

- If desired, use medium-grit sandpaper to distress the surface of the plaster, rubbing over the edges of the stripes to create an aged look (and to camouflage imperfections in the line). When you are finished rubbing back the color, wipe away the dust.

- Apply a coat of varnish to preserve your work. Allow the varnish to dry for 2 to 3 hours.

Despite the importance of carefully applying the tint to control the color line and degree of its saturation, tinting is an inexact science because of the chalkiness and porosity of the plaster substratum. You will quickly learn to appreciate the sun-washed effect and take joy in seeing the shifting shades of color.

PAPER AND TEXTILE COVERINGS

More commonly applied to bedroom walls than those in any other room, except perhaps in the dining room, **wallpaper** provides an efficient and dependable way to achieve the look of overall pattern, color, and style. Wallpaper is a also a glamorous way of concealing damaged walls. One note of caution: Always repair mars and holes in the wallboard before applying new wallpaper.

Although wallpaper comes in an infinite variety of designs, you may want a strong graphic like the striped pattern featured in a painted version on page 90. You can select from striped wallpapers that feature stripes in every imaginable color, width, and finish.

If you prefer a softer feel in bedroom wallpaper, like those articulated in pale colors and in fine prints, check out the wallpaper books that manufacturers make available in decorating stores to find designs that appeal to you. The bedroom featured above illustrates the feminine feel of going in this direction. Many manufacturers accompany their wallpapers with a line of textiles that match or coordinate with the featured papers. The value of such a broad offering is that it allows you to visually couple the stylistic sensibility of the walls and the soft furnishings in the room. The pairing results in a pleasing harmony of all the design elements in the room.

Always popular are the toile de Jouy patterns, rendered in sophisticated line drawings that depict country and court life, fantasy scenes, and wildlife configurations. For a romantic peacefulness, wallpaper in the English style is often preferred, chosen for its delicate depiction of country life printed in a repeat pattern. Particularly soothing in line and color is the toile de Jouy shown above. The wallpaper has a white ground with blue-colored designs. The other furnishings in the room key off its background color

and its feel of elegant simplicity. The predominate colorway of the room is quiet.

The luxury and beauty of a wall decked in **fabric** is unparalleled. Adding subtle texture and alluring softness, fabric is the perfect luxury material for wall covering in a bedroom. On the opposite page, a neoclassically styled bedroom is decorated in gray linen. The linen is subtly accented with decorative motifs that have been stenciled directly on the fabric in white fabric paint.

ABOVE

Fluffy pillows and the loft of a down comforter create an inviting atmosphere in this English country bedroom, papered with a delicate toile de Jouy pattern. The intricate pictorials on the wall coverings distract the eye from surprisingly spare furnishings.

OPPOSITE

A soothing palette of ivory, oatmeal, and gray unites the neoclassical elements in this grand bedroom. Forming the headboard of a majestic one-of-a-kind bed are architectural columns cut to size and a carved front panel from a piano. Two-inch-wide grosgrain ribbon outlines the creamy silk drapes and the bed skirt, and the luxurious medallions are hand stenciled in antique white, accenting the wall upholstered in textured linen.

Keep in mind that using fabric as a wall covering is a more serious undertaking than most other wall-decorating methods and is one that is best carried out with the help of a professional.

However, you can always test the technique on a smaller scale. For example, you can apply fabric to only one wall of the room, using paint or wallpaper to coordinate the remaining walls, especially those broken up by windows and doors where fitting the fabric is more daunting. The seams can be concealed with trim.

You can also use molding to frame large panels of fabric that coordinate with the room's furnishings. The simple steps are described in *Decking the Walls with Textiles* on page 25. The fabric panels can be made from lengths of toile de Jouy, usually made from a lightweight cotton and easier to affix. They can be made from luxurious needlepoint tapestries that depict scenes from an English garden. They can be also made from plain or embossed velvet or from brocades. The idea is to add texture to the central panels of each of the molding frames to create a dynamic play of color with the soft furnishings in the room.

FLOORS

If ceilings are relegated to an "out of sight out of mind" status and frequently ignored because of the physically arduous methods needed to change them, floors are by contrast regarded with near reverence, equal in importance to the walls of the bedroom. Hardwood floors are commonly covered with **wall-to-wall carpeting**, an expedient solution to adding warmth and comfort underfoot as well as color and pattern around. The carpet shown on page 112 is a fine example of a pattern that supports the more attention-grabbing design elements, its subtle coloration accented with woven brush strokes of color.

Although the wall-to-wall "solution" is common, it unwittingly conceals the beautiful wood floor, whereas showing off its natural patina and texture would clearly present a stronger design statement. The material that makes up the floor itself can underline the stylistic sense of the room and lend enormous charm and practical beauty. For example, the elegant charm of the floor in honeycomb-patterned terra-cotta **tiles** on page 93 and the brick floor laid in a herringbone pattern on page 111 illustrate the handsome efficiency of allowing the construction materials to show. The **painted floor** in the attic bedroom on page 103 illustrates a way of hiding in plain sight a common plywood floor while offering a pretty style solution.

You may want to combine the ideas of letting the natural floor show and adding textiles for warmth and interesting decorative accent. If so, consider laying down **area rugs** that leave some or most of the original floor in view. Position one area rug at each side of the bed to provide a cushion for the feet; then, if floor space allows, lay a larger area rug in the center of the floor. Don't hesitate to mix kilims and dhurries, or sisal carpets and sculpted Aubussons. Juxtaposing weaves and patterns set up an interesting decorating dynamic as illustrated in the bedroom featured on page 109, where braided rugs overlap on a small floor space.

CEILINGS

The easiest way to give new life to a bedroom is to paint the ceiling. A new color applied over a plain, unadorned ceiling can lift the chic quotient of the entire room. For a change from the traditional white, consider using **soft shades** of the wall color to provide an overall sweep of color, or using a paint color in stark contrast to the walls to dramatize each of these architectural features. Most paints are relatively dripless, cover easily, and dry quickly, so painting a ceiling is less stressful than it used to be.

If you are fortunate enough to have architectural details on your ceiling worth calling out, make an effort to highlight them in some way. Paint works particularly well. On the opposite page, the visual weight of an orderly configuration of thick beams forms the substantive ceiling in this spacious high-ceilinged, attic bedroom. Washed in a **diluted white paint** that resembles the effect of liming, the muscular rigor of the grain stands out while being subtle enough to blend with the soft pastel of the adjacent walls. On page 108, the sloping ceilings of this eave bedroom are made up of natural beams that are painted fancifully in an animal **print design**, connected by areas of smooth plaster. On page 107, a tent of **shirred fabric** forms a romantic ceiling canopy, further dressing up the tiny bedroom stuffed with textiles and soft furnishings.

OPPOSITE

The muscular struts of the wood beams meet plaster walls tinted a pale apple green in this first-floor bedroom. Striking is the clashing of patterned textiles that collude sympathetically on the hand-painted chest of drawers, the woven rug, and the bedspread. Adding touches of whimsy are a pair of sexy chairs (one is hiding behind the billowing sheer curtain) and an electric fan with propeller-style blades.

Lighting

Critical to inducing the yearned-for tranquillity and calm in the bedroom is modulating the quality and intensity of light as the functions of the bedroom change during the course of the day. Except at waking time, probably during the morning hours, the bedroom is usually unoccupied. If waking up to bright **sunshine** appeals to you, allow the light to blaze in, or filter it through translucent and patterned sheers to soften the glare, as seen on pages 98 and 102. An added benefit with patterned sheers is that the light throws the pattern stitched or printed on the fabric onto the floor. It is a lovely, if temporary, decorative effect.

If you prefer to wake up in slightly darkened room and also wish to ensure privacy both day and night, consider installing window **shades** or hanging lined **drapes** at each window. Although you can buy drapes in standard measurements to fit your windows or have them custom-made by a professional as shown on page 97, sewing simple drapes is easy, and you may want to try your hand at making them yourself. For more formal drapes, and for a more finished look, you can machine stitch a hem on the bottom edge of each panel, adding decorative fringe and tassel trim, if desired.

The bedroom at night depends on artificial sources of light. The most popular lighting, of course, is the **bedside lamps** seen in most of bedrooms featured in this chapter. Although many pairs of lamps are displayed on bedside tables and introduce a pleasing symmetry, single lamps with unique designs can also be displayed together. Look for lamps that sound the same stylistic note without being exact copies of one another. For example, consider the fringed shade pictured on the opposite page for inspiration.

Overhead lighting is used less commonly in the bedroom because most activities, including reading and sleeping, require low or spot lighting. Yet, there are exceptions:

Making a Window Covering

When using heavier fabrics to make more formal drapes, you may wish to apply the commercially available pleating tape and use the multipronged pins to make up neat vertical tucks in the fabric at the top of the drape. The technique is ostensibly foolproof. The simplest approach requires no sewing:

- Drape a swath of fabric—even an old but pretty silk bedspread or shawl—over a curtain rod, allowing the fabric to pool on the floor.

- Or, buy several yards of fabric, draping them over the top railing of a canopy bed to create mystery and coziness.

Consider those lighting fixtures that add style and panache to a bedroom. Although commonly associated with the more public spaces of the home, chandeliers are exquisitely romantic and elegant additions to any bedroom. The crystal chandelier featured on page 97 acts more like a piece of architecture than an actual source of light. When installed in the room and observed in daylight, the cut-crystal surfaces throw off shards of light and reflection.

OPPOSITE

In this country domain, daylight glows in the garden seen through nine-pane mullioned windows, while a mandarin-style lampshade disperses the warm glow of incandescent bulb. The standing lamp with a turned stem ends in the graceful curves of its pedestal base. The headboard of the iron bed with chipped paint is accented with a metal sculpture of a woman, carrying the style message of the hand-crocheted lace bedspread. A privacy screen covered in a romantic toile de Jouy creates a backdrop for a classic bronze bust that rests on the side table.

Furniture

To establish the atmosphere you dream of in your chic bedroom, begin furnishing the room with comfort in mind, especially when you are choosing the bed—the single, most important piece of furniture in the room. The bed serves as a visual focal point as well as the functional heart of the space.

Strictly speaking, the available floor space and the desired layout of the room will determine the size of the bed. It can be a single-sized box spring and mattress set on a frame in the corner of a garret or an expansive king-sized bed set on an ocean-sized French needlepoint carpet, as long as it provides a good night's sleep. Hence, choosing a mattress and box spring is the one place where money and care are invested well.

ABOVE

Soft textiles in plum and white tell the perfect bedtime story in this cottage bedroom. A patterned sheer sets the room aglow, and the floral print shade provides privacy. A textured woven bedspread, a duvet cover, and bed linen fall over one another on a pewter bed frame, while the soft hand of wool upholstery and the throw extend the cozy comfort of the room.

FAUX PAINT EFFECTS

Beds come in a vast array of styles and are made from a selection of durable materials, such as metal and wood. A particularly charming bed left *au naturel* is a brass bed with its highly polished surfaces. Demanding constant upkeep, brass beds are often dipped in a cleaner and then a sealed with a coat of protective varnish to reduce the need for extended care. A more practical bed material is iron, from which many turn-of-the-century bedsteads were made. Less expensive than brass, depending of course on the degree of ornamentation, iron beds are great candidates for a coat of **low-maintenance paint**. The iron bed on page 93 was painted lamp black, whereas the iron bed in the farmhouse bedroom on page 105 was painted white and then allowed to show the chips from wear and tear.

The basic method for producing chipped and peeling paint, also called **weathering**, usually begins with the application of water-based paint to the wood surfaces on your piece of furniture. For the look of chipped and peeling paint as illustrated on the three-drawer chest, use the method detailed in *Recreating the Look of Peeling Paint on Wood* on page 54. The availability of inexpensive wood furniture will encourage you to try your hand at creating the surface effects that artificially age and weather painted surfaces.

RIGHT

No attempt has been made to disguise the rough treatment and neglect of this three-drawer chest, which is a rich and spirited example of weathered paint. Matching the farmhouse chic style in this attic bedroom is an uphol-stered chair with a crackle finish, the worn, painted floor decorated in a diamond pattern, and the marred ochre paint on the metal garden urn. Mood lighting is provided by candlelight from a wall sconce and a bedside lamp with a whimsical striped lampshade. A more serious note is struck by oil paintings that stand sentry over the room.

 Recycling an Antique Bed

Be aware that if you purchase an antique metal bed, you may need to adapt a standard-sized mattress and box spring to a nonstandard bed frame, either by welding new pieces to keep the mattress and box spring in place or by using another creative solution. Before you paint a metal bed, you need to clean the metal surfaces of all grease and grime to prevent peeling. Thereafter, you can use a soft brush to apply several coats of paint in the desired color, allowing the paint to dry between coats.

The **crackle finish** is the perfect faux effect for artificially weathering and aging furniture of any style, especially if you wish to establish a farmhouse-chic style in your bedroom. You can move confidently toward saturated color, especially the palette of the 1950s, an era of turquoise, robin's egg blue, salmon pink, and mint green. When these colors are expressed in a group of humble furnishings treated to the crackle finish—especially primitively made cupboards, chairs, and beds—the effect is at once eclectic and emotionally reassuring. The straightforward honesty of this style makes it appealing and, most important, makes it easy for you to replicate pieces that have become expensive to buy.

To reproduce the crackle effect so characteristic of the farmhouse chic in your bedroom, simply think in terms of anything that sends off signals of spirit-soothing comfort and peacefulness of a farm in the 1950s. Perhaps the recognition of and the associations with a simpler time are what cause you to gravitate toward this look. Nevertheless, if you want to accomplish it, in practical terms, you need to choose pieces of furniture, especially wood items, that are plainly constructed, especially the inexpensive wood "blanks" upon which you can apply several faux paint effects. The faux crackle finish creates a convincing historical reference to actual origins of some wood furniture. Subjected to the wear and tear of normal use, the effects of humidity and the weather when the pieces were carelessly stored in damp cellars or barns or even left out in the elements, farmhouse furniture depends upon these textural infractions for their authenticity and value.

You can unify all you find in one bedroom setting, using coats of white paint on furniture treated with a crackle medium. Or you can introduce furniture painted and crackled in outrageously glamorous colors, like turquoise or orange, placing these so-called attention getters among the more subdued pieces painted white or cream.

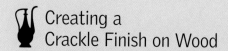

Creating a Crackle Finish on Wood

One way to age and add character to wood is to create a crackle finish as featured on the French-style chair on page 103.

- First remove any upholstery, and wipe down the carved wood frame.

- Then, apply a premixed coat of latex paint in creamy white or another desired color. Let the paint dry for a few hours. Then, apply a thin coat of crackle varnish over the painted surfaces.

- Work the brush in the direction in which you want to see the crackle lines appear: horizontal strokes for horizontal crazes or cracks, and vertical strokes for vertical crazes or cracks.

- For a more pronounced look, you can apply a second contrasting top coat. When it dries, cracks and crazes will appear more pronounced.

- To further antique the crackle finish, rub burnt sienna glaze into the cracks.

Textural finishes are used to treat a piece of furniture overall, and it is the texture that draws the eye. By contrast, there are paint effects that create pattern and confer the look of rare and expensive materials, rare woods like ebony and bird's eye maple, and natural materials like tortoiseshell and amber, all of which require experience to reproduce. Nevertheless, there are fun shortcuts that result in convincing copies or fantasy versions of the prized materials that charm. The bamboo secretary on page 108 shows the tortoiseshell pattern, created nonchalantly using bursts of color from a can of black spray paint, for example.

Although broad technical approaches to recreating authentic wood grains and surface textures can include using spray

paint and commercial preparations, some painted effects require diligence and experience to achieve. A primary example is **trompe l'oeil**, a painting style that creates the illusion that you are looking at an actual object or scene, when in fact you are seeing a near-photographically accurate copy of the object, meticulously rendered in paint. The perceptual trick is based on technical skill and demands both talent and experience. However, there are levels of visual "fraud" that are perfectly acceptable and appealing. Even though your efforts may produce less-than-realistic representations, you can still enjoy the process of creating stylized versions of trompe l'oeil illusions. A range of trompe l'oeil work is featured in the bedroom on page 107, where parrot tulips decorate entry doors, as well as on the armoire on page 112 where you get a glimpse of a garden vista through parted drapes.

ABOVE

Flowers are the subtle theme carried throughout this country chic bedroom, crowded with unabashedly humble things whose vintage sensibilities stir memories of summer mornings—simple roses form a medallion on a chenille bedspread, a reassuring textile from the 1950s; a blanket in a geranium-red floral print covers the base of an iron bed, spruced up with a coat of white paint; frameless oil paintings rendered in the last century depict homegrown asters in a vase and a field of daisies. An old floor cupboard in robin's egg blue is called into new service as a makeshift dresser. Showing the effects of dampness and use, a crackle finish has crazed the paint.

ABOVE

A cheerful mix of antique and modern furniture fills this sunny bedroom painted a bright yellow. A patchwork-style woven rug displays huge garden vegetables in bold graphics and leads the eye to a pair of modern metal chairs finished in a glossy cardinal red. The centuries' old armoire made of pine has simple lines and a distinct, utilitarian sensibility relieved by the decoration that adorns the piece. Hand painted in the folk art style of last century's Scandinavian artists, the emphatic strokes have left bold, leafy swirls applied in mirror images on the doors and sides of the piece.

Another fine example of using paint is apparent in the free-hand **folk painting** on the simple pine armoire featured on the opposite page. If you are confident with an artist's paint-brush, you can decorate the front panels of ordinary wood doors and the drawers or contours of bedroom furniture using acrylic paint, referring to the photograph on the opposite page for inspiration. You can also use stencils to reproduce primitive folk art design, enhancing the design with additional details painted freehand.

EMBELLISHMENTS

When treating your furniture to a faux effect, keep the small details in mind to make the entire piece consistent in age and style. For example, if you antique a dresser, don't forget to choose **hardware** in period-compatible designs. Also, antique the hardware so that it doesn't stand out as brand-new. Glazes and shoe polish can be used to suggest accumulated **grime** in knobs and hinges, as illustrated by the porcelain knobs on the dresser shown on page 105.

To add **period detail** to new wood pieces, especially flat wood panels like those found on wooden headboards, foot-boards, and drawer fronts, add carved bows and flowers or any other decorative motifs to create textural interest and period detailing. These embellishments are easy to apply, a simple matter of securing resin reproductions in position using white glue, followed by an overall coat or two of paint to homogenize all the elements.

ABOVE

Slender doors, decorated with hand-painted botanicals trompe l'oeil style, provide an intimate glimpse into this bedroom that is lush with textiles. The walls are covered in shirred fabric in pale berry and cream-colored stripes, and the ceiling is tented with a coordinated fabric in salmon, forming a canopy. A rich, red-and-green print is trimmed in fringe and forms the bed valance, and an upholstered headboard is covered in a tufted chintz featuring large palm fronds on a salmon field.

Soft Furnishings

The use of fabrics to accent or change the look of the furniture in your bedroom is one of the most practical ways to revitalize or change completely the appearance and stylistic sensibility of the room. Whereas professionals can swoop into the room, measure and plan, and then bring back the most exuberantly beautiful soft furnishings you have ever imagined, you will find that some upholstery processes, although moderately difficult, can be accomplished at home. If you want to make a soft furnishing of some sort, begin with a small project.

WINDOW TREATMENTS

When windows and furniture in the bedroom are dressed in faded old fabrics, they take on an approachable gallantry and elegance that only draping textiles can confer. Beginning with the windows, because they often require some covering for privacy, consider the near-instant approach to **drapes**, that of laying a swath of fabric over a curtain rod. The fabric can run rod to floor, or it can be a nonchalantly tossed scarf. Experiment by mixing and matching vintage prints coordinated by color or pattern. Suspend panels of **sheer fabric** or **embroidered lace** over a painted dowel, and tack it over a window.

Drapes can also be used to majestic effect when they cascade from a **coronne** placed above the headboard near the ceiling. Also called **corona drapes**, these drapes can be folded over a pole extended from and fixed to the wall. The drapes are made in the same way as loose drapes for windows. The only difference is that the lining is the same width as the outside fabric, so when viewed from inside the bed, they appear neatly tailored. The drapes can be made of sheer fabric that filters light; upholstery-weight fabric, such as a brocade or velvet; or a lighter fabric, such as silk or cotton chintz. These drapes are usually tucked behind tiebacks at opposite sides of the headboard.

Although drapes are naturally associated with windows, drapes can also be used to establish the integrity of a space, especially in a one-room living situation as featured on the opposite page. These ruffled panels dress up a really raw space and provide much-needed privacy.

BEDS AND CHAIRS

Upholstery can add chic style and plump sensuality to any bedroom. **Headboards** and **footboards** can be cocooned in fabric that matches the textiles in the room. **Chairs** can be recovered with a hodgepodge of vintage fabrics. The principles of upholstering furniture of different style and character change subtly from piece to piece, but the technique generally involves padding the skeleton of the item and covering the padding with a decorative fabric to reveal the contours, as illustrated by the headboard on page 107. Consult a professional for perfect work right off the bat.

LEFT

A veritable jungle of animal prints is lavished on the furnishings in this spacious attic bedroom. A delicate settee with a carved frame is painted white and upholstered in a tufted cheetah animal print, striking a stylistic paradox with the snob appeal of the settee. The ordinary wood bed is painted white, its footboard sporting a plush, leopard lap throw with accent pillows made up in the markings of a fantasy winter leopard, with ceiling beams painted to match. A nearby bamboo secretary is camouflaged in a fantasy faux tortoiseshell.

Making a Pillow

With as little as one-half yard of fabric, you can make a simple pillow.

- To begin, buy a square pillow form.

- Use its measurement plus an inch or so to cut two squares.

- Put the squares together, wrong sides facing, and machine stitch all four sides, leaving an opening for turning.

- Clip the corners.

- Turn the case right side out, and stuff in your pillow form.

- Slipstitch the opening closed.

Using this simple construction, you can make the animal print pillows featured on the opposite page and most other pillows seen in this chapter. For extra chic styling, add trims, tassels, and beads.

Aging Fabric

If you are looking for unique sources of exotic textiles and want to avoid cut yard goods when you jazz up your bedroom, consider using Indian saris, adding sequins and tassels to accent the edges. If you have new fabric in colors that are glaringly bright and too new-looking to fit into your vintage space, simulate the look of aged fabric by dunking it in a bath of tea or coffee. The light brown stain will quiet down the colors and age the appearance of the fabric without obliterating the pattern or texture.

PILLOWS

Home-sewn accessories, especially **pillows**, are not only easy to do, they provide the emotional pleasure and stylistic punctuation that can catalyze the elements in the faux chic bedroom. By using some imagination and having a clear understanding of what you want in your bedroom, you can transform a ho-hum room that puts you to sleep to one that wakes you up.

ABOVE

A bohemian mix of fabrics in curry yellow and dove gray decorate this sliver of a bedroom in a studio apartment. The curtains are made in a cotton print, a simple case of machine stitching a gathered strip to one side of a panel of fabric; the bed is piled high with a down comforter, blankets, and pillows, tempting visitors to crawl in. The ruffle of lace decorating the edge of the shelf is worn and dusty, but it fits in with the gypsy sensibility of the entire space, which is accented with colonial-style braided rugs.

Sewing a Lap Throw

Making a lap throw is a fine example of a project that provides enormous pleasure. Smaller than blankets, lap throws are absolutely the easiest soft furnishing to make, even if you are a beginner. All you do is measure and cut two large rectangles of fabric, such as velvet, low-pile cotton, or wool flannel. Each type of fabric has a nice hand and sews up easily. Put the rectangles together, wrong sides facing, and use a sewing machine to stitch around all four sides, leaving an opening for turning. Clip the corners, turn the throw right side out, and slip stitch the opening closed. Of course, you can also add fancy trims or tassels to the edges and corners, according to your taste. When you are finished, simply curl up with a good book and your lap throw.

Of course, you can always make soft furnishings for your bedroom on a modest scale. The ideas and simple directions below should get you started. For more detailed directions, consult the sewing books in "Sources and Resources" on page 139.

BELOW

The aristocratic elegance of this extraordinary French-style bedroom is expressed foremost in the carved and gilded coronne from which the sweeping lengths of the silk bed drapes cascade to the headboard, which is carved, painted, gilded, and upholstered in silk. A crocheted bedspread and zebra print throw share the top of the bed, at whose foot is a roll-neck chaise upholstered in pale, leaf green damask, accented by a floral chintz pillow with silk fringe. A pair of urn-shaped lamps with a crackle finish rest on matching bedside tables with marble tops, curvaceous legs ornately carved and painted in 18th-century style.

Making a Simple Cushion

Another easy project is to make a cushion to soften the seat of an otherwise hard bench. You can make one in a fabric that matches the room's textiles, as featured above, where a wrought-iron bench situated at the end of the bed has a custom-fit cushion that matches the bedspread.

- Measure the seat of your bench, and use the measurement to cut two pieces of your chosen fabric.

- With right sides facing and all edges together, machine stitch the four sides, leaving a small opening for turning.

- Clip the corners, turn the case right side out, and stuff it with fiberfill.

- Slip stitch the opening closed.

A rustic attic bedroom is dressed in gentle swaths of white fabric— a *boutis* hand quilted in undulating patterns, bed linen edged in crocheted lace, and sheer drapes falling from the cathedral ceiling to the headboard below. Keeping the light-enhancing theme going are the plaster walls painted white and the beams washed in white paint. Modern art—a witty urn sculpture made from chicken wire, a folk art doll, a wire mesh ball— decorate the room. Adding curves and lines are the wrought-iron bar chair and a settee, each painted black. Light from a floor-level window illuminates the tall, wooden carving painted black and white and the rough-hewn blocks of stone laid in a herringbone pattern.

Decorative Accessories

The bedroom is a space that encourages you to collect great accessories that serve your needs for creature comfort and emotional satisfaction. It has already been said that sets of lamps, pairs of area rugs, and the like are traditionally chosen, serving the room's partners equally. But it is in the spirit of chic style that you choose single, fabulous, "must-have" accessories about which you dream and obsess—a one-of-a-kind **lamp with a beaded fringe**, a woven rug in fuchsia, a **frame encrusted with rhinestones**, an occasional chair covered in a full-blown Victorian rose print. After all, these are the accessories worth having, the decorative elements that inspire your passions. Although you may require your accessories to serve specific needs—little lamps light your bedside tables, **area rugs** cushion your feet—accessories certainly serve more than functional purposes: They reveal your deepest emotional and aesthetic inclinations.

Look at the accessories that decorate the bedroom pictured on the right. There is no mistaking the personality and style revealed in the arrangements. If you are interested in placing just the right accessory in your bedroom, be on the lookout for it everywhere, not just in retail stores and boutiques. Haunt flea markets, check out tag sales, visit local artisans when you travel to exotic places. Just keep looking until an accessory speaks to you, and then get it. In this way, you will be able to look around your bedroom and find evidence of yourself and your loved ones, and you will sleep and wake in good company.

ABOVE

The whimsical fantasy of this bedroom could have been taken from the pages of *Alice in Wonderland*, where a personal collection of favorite things introduces a beguiling clutter of patterns and styles. Covered in a sweet, ribbon-patterned wallpaper, the walls are hung with rather serious hand-tinted prints from the last century, but romantic chaos reigns in the floral chintz and animal-print fabrics that decorate the pillows on a stuffed pink chair outlined in black piping and on the curvaceous ottoman tricked out in tassels and painted in a faux-leopard pattern. An improbable armchair carved in a fish shape shares attention with a marble table with a fish base and an openwork tote encrusted with plastic charms. The doors of the armoire are painted in a stylized trompe l'oeil, offering a balcony view of a formal garden; the top is stacked ceiling high with decorated hatboxes.

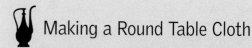

Making a Round Table Cloth

Tablecloths are another soft furnishing that can add striking color and style to your bedroom. If you have a small round table that is sturdy but unpresentable as is, make a tablecloth like the one featured on page 95. Note that because the width of the tablecloth will probably exceed the normal width of cut yard goods, you will need to piece the cloth from several separate sections. Sew enough fabric together so that you can form a large circle that covers your tabletop, hangs over the edge, and touches the floor.

Collectibles

The bedroom is the perfect place to crowd in collectibles and mementos of the most personal nature—**framed photographs** can fill a dresser top, along with cut-crystal perfume **bottles** and a brush and handheld **mirror set** inherited from a favorite grandmother. Although your favorite things might be items you can hold, personal loves are often reflected in the **linen** you keep. Fine handwork from a generation when sewing was thought of as an aristocratic art should be brought out from storage and laid over canopies and dressers. Lace and cutwork can be adapted for use as dresser scarves, if you want to appreciate the filigree of amazingly ornate stitches that form the curling monograms and intricate stitches rendered in complicated floral borders.

Beds can sag under the weight of needlepoint **pillows**, and favorite **books** can form wobbly towers on night tables and carpeted floors. If you are unsure of what to do with a humble collection of vintage canning **jars**, fill them with riot of wildflowers picked from your garden or purchased from a farm stand or corner deli, and march them down a long windowsill. If you love **framed art**, use it to configure a kind of headboard over a plain bed.

ABOVE

A collection of framed art paves the wall behind a plain bed, unwittingly forming an impromptu headboard. Pictures that have not found their place on the wall lean casually against the louvered door of a built-in wall unit. Piles of bed pillows are dressed in stark white cotton, edged in hand-crocheted lace. A perfect setting for a snoozing cat, the bed billows with a welcoming down quilt.

The Bathroom

THE BATHROOM IS ONE OF THE MOST PERSONAL AND PRIVATE INTERIOR SPACES OF ANY home. Although its primary purpose is to provide for the care of your most basic and intimate needs, it is more than that. It is a space in which you can escape to restore your balance and revitalize your senses. Hence, the chic style in this room springs, most often, from a kind of practical aestheticism where you choose furnishings and accessories that simultaneously fulfill your needs and support your moods, while doing a particular task.

Practically speaking, most bathrooms come supplied with the requisite trio of plumbing fixtures—the sink, toilet, and tub—regardless of the size of the room (with the exception of the guest bathroom, which might contain only a sink and toilet). Thereafter, the room is typically decorated with any and all items that cleanse, soothe, and rejuvenate—from thick, soft towels made of Egyptian cotton, to a flowing shower curtain made from French cutwork, to lotions and elixirs infused with botanical fragrances, to a privacy screen that encloses you in a pool of soothing water. As you peruse the photos in this chapter, consider applying the faux effects to your bathroom space.

General information on selected faux effects has been provided and is noted with this icon. However, be sure to consult "Sources and Resources" on pages 139 to 141 for more detailed information that will help ensure professional-looking results and provide important working safeguards.

Faux Effects for Architectural Elements

WALLS

The walls are one of the most prominent architectural elements in the bathroom. Whether made of a material that can stand up to the effects of humidity and water or treated to resist these effects, the walls can be covered in paint, paper, or tile.

FAUX PAINT EFFECTS

The **color** and pattern used to decorate the walls in the bathroom can be bold and vibrant. Although the fixtures may present one colorway, the walls can be painted in a different colorway, as illustrated on page 114. In this small guest bathroom, a strong graphic stripe enlarges the sense of space and makes the other elements in the room recede. The striped pattern is created using the method described on page 18.

The **patterns** on your bathroom walls can also be busy like those found on the sloping walls of the bathroom on page 131. The overall pattern was first planned on paper and then blocked out in chalk on the walls. Dependent on repeat motifs, the complex mix of shapes and subtle color creates a soft backdrop for the tub, rendered in more vivid graphic detail in a similar colorway.

FAUX TEXTURAL EFFECTS

Many bathrooms constructed in the last century have plaster walls. At the time of construction, the material is typically treated with a sealer to prevent the effects of water and humidity from marring its surface. However, even diligent efforts are ineffective against the natural flaking and crumbling that occur once plaster has been subjected to moisture. Despite this, plaster walls are still being constructed and treated to interesting surface decoration. The material itself has properties that make it an ideal substrate for the textural effects you might otherwise have difficulty

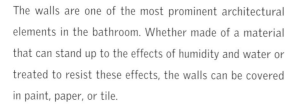

Painting Faux Tile

On the opposite page, a plaster wall in a large bathroom has been decorated in a checkerboard pattern. Stylized by the "scribbling" brushwork, the pattern is easy to reproduce.

- First, map out the grid of squares in paint, using lines snapped on with a chalk-laden string.
- Then, fill in each marked square with blue paint, holding the loaded brush firmly but keeping the wrist flexible as it scribbles on color, creating the distinct lines of overlapping color. The overall effect simulates the look of large tiles.

This faux effect is an appealing, stylized substitute for laying real tile on the wall. Unless the plaster wall is perfectly flat and smooth, using ceramic tile is inadvisable.

reproducing on walls made of nonporous materials. Plaster's natural chalky character and porosity affect the absorption of paint applied to its surface, creating a **mottling of color** and textural effects that are unique and beautiful.

OPPOSITE

A shower hoop holds a softly gathered curtain, accented in French cutwork, that cascades over the edge of a footed tub with a sensual contour. Decorated in a painterly style, its faux finish is rendered in blue on its exterior sides, the same blue color that fills the oversized grid of squares that forms a checkerboard pattern on the walls. A bamboo occasional table and an antique full-length mirror provide additional creature comfort, as do the appliquéd hand towels hanging from decorative brass rings on the marble tabletop custom fit with a round porcelain sink. A little footstool picks up the checkerboard pattern in a pink-and-white pillowcase that covers its cushion.

PAPER COVERINGS

Walls in the bathroom can be decorated using **wallpaper** as long as the wall has been prepared ahead of time. It is important to clean the walls and to treat them to a mold-retardant wash to prevent mold from forming on the applied paper and causing stains and buckling. It is also important to use an adhesive on the back of the wallpaper that holds up to humidity. Poor bonding glue will allow moisture to lift and curl the paper away from the wall. Wallpaper for the bathroom is often made of vinyl for this reason. Its surface is sealed against the effects of water and humidity, slowing the deleterious effects of water absorption.

However, you need not feel compelled to go the absolutely practical route, using **vinyl papers** that can be unattractively shiny. When choosing paper, select paper with a design and colorway that is pleasing to you. Foremost, you need to like the paper if you are to live with it peacefully.

If your bathroom is well-ventilated, you can pretty much apply whatever wallpaper suits your tastes, with the caveat that moisture will be a constant foil, so consider papering sections of walls, such as those away from a source of water.

The bathroom on the opposite page illustrates the use of wallpaper to strong, graphic effect. Among a decidedly funky set of decorative elements, the rigid pattern of this wallpaper is a nice counterpoint to the softer lines and quirkiness of the other accessories. The strong horizontal rows of rectangles simulate the look of European **stone blocks** seen on old city buildings. Together with the eccentric though practical mix of decorations, the room holds together in a kind of Left Bank chic way, with each decorative accessory serving a particular function—a weathered garden chair serves as seating, a small demi-lune shelf near the sink holds cosmetic necessities, and a weathered frame of chicken wire covers the base of the tub.

Painting Stone Blocks

The stone block pattern can be applied to walls in your bathroom.

- To create the template for one block, photocopy the page, enlarging one block as desired.

- Use the pattern to cut a stencil from Mylar or cardboard the weight of a manila folder.

- Once the pattern is cut, use a stencil brush and a bouncing motion to apply the paint to the cutouts.

The texture of the decorative border should appear light and grainy.

OPPOSITE

In this Left Bank chic bathroom, an eccentric collision of style creates impact and dynamism. Framed family photos, a mirror with an elegant frame, and a unique tub frame of weathered board and chicken wire conspire to upset the order established by the faux stone block wallpaper. Plumbing fixtures are left exposed, along with a water-damaged chair constructed from wood slats. A ceiling light is an inverted, conically shaped lampshade that illuminates a demi-lune shelf near the porcelain sink. Odd area rugs overlap on the floor, giving this bathroom a nonchalance and lived-in look.

Decorating the walls of the bathroom can include the use of **fine art**. On the opposite page, a tropical theme is elegantly carried out in a luxurious bathroom fitted with mirrors that run from the ceiling to the countertop. Between the mirrors, panels of **painted paper** are positioned, each panel depicting an aspect of the lush life lived in a faraway tropical place, rendered in watercolor. The interesting thing to note is that at first glance the art appears to be made up of separate pieces. On closer inspection, the art reveals itself to be a long panel applied to the wall in a vertical orientation. Strips of **decorative molding** that have divided up the panel create the illusion of separate framed images. The molding is stained the same warm brown as the lustrous countertop. A pane of glass protects the art, but it is important to note that the featured bathroom might not be well used, because original art can be damaged and devalued by the marring effects of humidity. In addition, glass can add substantial weight to the wall, and it must be anchored properly. Consult an expert for help in setting up your own **framed murals**, in order to avoid any safety hazards.

 ## Creating Framed Murals

If you are interested in simulating the look of the bathroom on the opposite page, you need not find original art, of course. Instead, you can find reproduction prints and posters and wallpaper murals to create the same effect.

- Look for images that can be pieced together to form an aesthetic whole, whether a scene or a set of coordinated designs or motifs. Especially versatile are the depictions of sprawling landscapes used on wallpaper murals.

- Cut and configure the murals to fit your space.

- Use wallpaper paste to adhere each image to the wall, making certain you smooth the paper to eliminate air bubbles. If you inadvertently discover an air bubble, prick the paper with a pin, and press down on the paper to allow the air to escape. (Notice the hole "disappears.")

- Smooth over the paper with a stiff nylon brush.

The framing can be achieved using wood molding as shown. For helpful advice, consult an expert, especially when forming the mitered corners of the frames. This little detail can make an important difference in creating an overall look and ensuring a professional-looking finish. You can also apply the many faux finishes to the wood molding, using a painted effect to create a chipped and peeling finish. For a weathered look, use a stain technique or rubbed-in white paint, rubbing off the excess so that only the grain takes the color.

FLOORS

Most bathroom floors are constructed from tile or some other hard, waterproof material. Although they are usually left bare of any covering, **small accent rugs** may be used to add color and pattern, while at the same time providing a soft cushion underfoot, especially near the tub and the sink.

These small accents can be decoratively unobtrusive, like **bath mats** that coordinate with towels. However, they can also be decorative centerpieces that congeal the decorating theme you have established with the other statements made on walls or through your plumbing fixtures. In the sleek, black-and-white bathroom on the opposite page, a **large area rug** carries out the clean lines and the colorway set up in the room. Its pattern resembles a chevron pattern seen through a kaleidoscope. The rug draws the eye and calls attention to the other decorative elements in the room that have the same black detailing—from the sensual lines of the iron chair to the framed black-and-white line drawings on the far wall.

For another look at area rugs as decorative accent, consider the bathroom on page 119. Treated more nonchalantly, the **overlapping rugs** appear to be more of an afterthought. Perhaps drawn from other venues, the rugs provide cushioning and color. The casual accents appear to have been laid down to provide safe footing, but they also carry out the decorating approach used throughout the room, which basically involves using what is available as long as it serves a useful purpose or adds panache and personality.

CEILINGS

The ceiling in a bathroom tends to play little role in the over-all decorating scheme of a typical cube-shaped bathroom, except to contain ductwork for heating or air condition-ing or to hold a light fixture. The exception would be in those bathrooms where there is a sloping ceiling, like those found in attics and eaves.

Because the wall heights in those kinds of rooms are lower, many lack a traditional window; hence, **skylights** often come into play, providing not only ambient light and air circulation but also a panoramic view of the changing sky. Such an architectural feature also provides interest-ing visual geometry that can be played out in other straight lines and uncluttered spaces. Such is the case with the bath-room on page 122 where line and contour play strong dec-orative roles. By contrast, the bathroom skylight on page 131 forms a visual relief in a sloped ceiling that is patterned in hand-painted Santa Fe colors. Interestingly, the room is quite uncluttered in terms of actual furniture. When seen from a broad perspective, the skylight forms a bright rectangle of light against the simple geometry of the tub and a few soft accessories.

Lighting

Overall, the bathroom is commonly designed with overhead lighting installed in the ceiling. Mirrored walls often reflect the light, acting as adjunct lighting. Although practical, such lighting sources are usually unflattering, especially to the natural tones of the skin, and are antithetical to creating a soothing atmosphere. For this reason, you may want to install more individual sources of light, including dimmers on spot lighting, so that you can create more intimacy and warmth. On page 120, a ceiling **chandelier** and **wall sconces** illuminate an aristocratically styled bathroom. The chandelier throws off low light and casts a romantic shadow on the ceiling. The sconces are fitted with pretty shades, coverings that further filter the light in the room and add a sense of drama.

These romantic effects can be created using **small lamps** and other spot lighting, even **candles**. Candlelight in the bathroom immediately establishes a mood of calm and serenity. Of course, you must observe certain safety precautions when using candles with open flames. For example, never leave a lighted candle unattended, always keep candles away from flammable materials and out of the reach of children and pets, and always use care when handling candles, especially if they have been burning for a while, because melted wax can burn your skin.

That said, consider candles for your guest bathroom or your master bathroom. Candles come in a wide variety of shapes, sizes, colors, and styles. The most common candles are pillar candles. Smooth and rodlike in shape, pillar candles are available in circumferences large enough to provide a stable base. They are relatively inexpensive, and they often come in versions that emit soothing, botanical fragrances.

 ## Etching a Glass Votive

Etching can turn a plain votive candleholder into an elegant one in a matter of minutes. Simply follow these easy steps:

- Plan to do the etching in a well-ventilated room. Then, clean a drinking tumbler, making sure you remove all grease and fingerprints.

- Cut leaf shapes from masking tape or Frisket, and apply them to the side of the glass, pressing down the edges with the back of a spoon.

- Put on protective rubber gloves and safety glasses; the etching cream is toxic. Then use a sponge brush to apply etching cream to all exposed glass.

- Wait ten minutes, and then wash off the cream and peel away the tape.

- Wash and dry the glass, and then place a votive inside.

OPPOSITE

Reflected in a sparkling Venetian mirror is a variety of votive candles—small glasses with gilt and painted designs, a frosted chimney with etching and its counterpart, a drinking tumbler with a delicately etched swag. A candlestick with a hoop shade hung with crystal drops dominates the arrangement, while a small, flared votive perched on a glass candlestick stands sentry at the far end of the arrangement.

Another common candle style that works well in the bathroom is the **votive**, a small candle placed inside a flameproof container usually made of ceramic or glass. The glass containers can be decorated with designs using a quick **etching** process. The technique allows you to cut simple geometric shapes from tape or Frisket, which is a translucent **self-adhesive film**, and apply them in a pretty configuration to the side of any clean glass. When an etching cream is applied to the exposed glass, it degrades the surface of the glass and gives the glass a frosted look. The containers can also be made from cut crystal. The flickering light from the flame casts beautiful refracted light when it passes through the crystal, decorating nearby surfaces with interesting light patterns. Set several votive candles along a shelf. Place one on the sill of the tub.

Candles and sachets can also help create a home spa environment. Candles that have aromatherapeutic properties, such as natural eucalyptus and rose, have pleasing scents. These, and many other scents, are also available in oils, usually made from a combination of the essential oil of the particular scent and a neutral, nonfragrant carrier oil, like almond oil. These oils can be used to scent potpourri placed in a ceramic dish, or they can be drizzled on the bathwater for a relaxing environment. Sachets are a perfect solution to infusing a subtle fragrance in closed spaces, such as closets and drawers.

Fixtures

The fixtures in a bathroom are vital to its functioning and so may simply be considered "furniture." In some ways, like wood furniture, the **ceramic fixtures** in your bathroom can be treated to accents and other decorative effects, assuming you use special ceramic paint for porcelain surfaces. Use a watercolor brush to add simple flowers and leaves to single tiles.

Or for an easy decorative idea that is especially suited to the old **cast-iron tubs**, you can add color and pattern to its exterior portions, which are usually exposed and crudely finished. The claw-footed tub on page 117 is a fine example of an overall **sponge technique**.

Making a Sachet

- Make a miniature pillowcase from scraps of leftover fabric.

- Sprinkle lavender buds on a handful of fiberfill, roll it up, and stuff it into the case.

- Sew the opening of the case closed.

- Add a ribbon, and hang the sachet on a hanger, or place it in your lingerie drawer or in your linen closet.

RIGHT

An oval washbasin with exposed plumbing sits on a stone slab situated between two walls in this small bathroom. A high window with a privacy shade provides light, as do two cut-crystal chandeliers hung overhead. A pair of rearview, truck-style mirrors add witty counterpoint to this functional space.

Although technically not furniture, **shelving and storage** are necessary for keeping things neat and orderly. They are especially key to organizing additional towels and toiletries. You can use **baskets**, stacking them on a shelf, or you can add **towel racks** and **hooks**. These fixtures come in metal, wood, glass, and combinations of these materials. If your bathroom style is squeaky clean with straight lines, you may wish to bring in gleaming chrome and glass, setting an **étagère** against a wall and showing off your bath linen in neatly folded stacks.

Painting a Cast-Iron Tub

Painting the exterior of a cast-iron tub is easy, but it is important to prepare the surface before you apply the ground color and the decorative patterns, especially if your tub is a found treasure from a salvage dealer.

- Scrub the interior porcelain using a mild abrasive cream.

- For the exterior, use a wire brush to remove any flaking paint.

- Remove any rust spots with steel wool, then wash the surface with grime-busting soap and water.

- Apply a coat of rust inhibitor followed by a coat of metal primer to all exterior surfaces, allowing the paint to dry overnight.

- Finally, use an oil-based undercoat and oil-based decorative paints.

RIGHT

The most striking feature of this attic bathroom is the broad mix of pattern and motif that decorates the ceiling and the bathtub. The variety of graphic motifs deceives you into thinking that this room is cluttered, when it is, in reality, a simple open space surprisingly spare of furnishing. A skylight forms a clean rectangle of light in a angled ceiling decorated in a soft yellow pattern, accented by a scalloped fabric where the wall and ceiling meet. The shapes and patterns play off the broad graphic on the bathtub, artfully painted with diamond shapes and mythical birds.

Making a Bath Throw

Instead of a bathrobe, wrap yourself in an oversized bath throw made from an absorbent, washable fabric like terry cloth or 100 percent cotton plush in an animal print, as pictured on the opposite page. To make your own throw, follow these basic steps:

- Measure and cut two large rectangles of fabric.
- Lay them together, right sides facing.
- Then, machine stitch all four sides, leaving an opening for turning.
- Turn the blanket (or throw) to the right side and stitch up the opening.

OPPOSITE

This classically styled bathroom is filled with soft furnishings and accessories in a surprising, contemporary style. Made to set a stylistic counterpoint, the items are designed to indulge the body and soothe the spirit. Against a subtle emerald green wall painted in a striated pattern stands a vibrant, black-and-white paneled screen that provides added privacy at the tub. A low lady's chair is upholstered in fresh English chintz and has tufted back and shirred seat detailing. A velvet pillow in green and magenta works together with a lap quilt in an animal print to provide surprisingly exotic accent, together with a custom-fit pillow in a matching zebra pattern outlined in black, brush fringe.

Soft Furnishings

With the basic "furniture" in the guise of the fixtures in place, decorating the bathroom is about soft furnishings, those essential elements that support your bathing and personal-care rituals—thick **towels** and **mats** that are textured and colorful, a **shower curtain** that flows from an overhead rod, a minimally **draped window**, items that serve you and soften the hard-edged sensibility of the bathroom space.

There are other appealing ways to establish comfort and relaxation, and if you have the space, it is well worth considering a **plump chair** on which to sit, an absorbent **lap throw**, and a **soft pillow** to indulge your senses.

If you want to do some home sewing, there are easy soft furnishings for the bathroom. If you have a small, upholstered chair, you can add a **washable slipcover**. Or you can simply drape a pretty towel or lap throw over an arm. Follow the directions for making a pillow and a lap quilt found on pages 109 and 110 in the bedroom chapter, or review the basic principles here. For the minimal seating, and if space allows, bring a small chair or stool into the room, especially one with a inset seat cushion. It is easy to change the look of the fabric that covers the seat base by covering it with new fabric. The same fabric can also be used to make new panels for a room screen as shown on the opposite page.

Decorative Accessories

The single, most important accessory in the bathroom is the **mirror**. It is the one furnishing that is essential to carrying out your daily rituals. Although the mirrors in old bathrooms were ordinarily attached to the door of a medicine cabinet, today's mirrors are often independent decorations. What makes the mirror an appealing accessory is that it creates an illusion of a larger room. The mirror is also a style statement, typically expressed in the frame that surrounds the center glass. The **frame** on the mirror can be manipulated to express a distinct sense of style and period, from **gleaming gold**, to **brushed steel**, to **stained** and **carved wood**. The frame can carry out the style messages already established by the other fixtures in the room, or it can introduce an eye-riveting change.

If the idea of creating your own framed mirror is appealing to you, visit flea markets and tag sales for a structurally sound picture frame in a style of your choice.

Then, after you have treated it with a faux finish, have a mirror custom cut to fit the frame, making certain the mirror is set securely.

Accessories can also include items that add fragrance to the room while adding color and texture—pretty bottles filled with lotions and splashes, scented soaps, and fresh flowers.

Making Potpourri

A simple mixture of dried flowers or wood shavings and a few drops of essential oil are all that you need to make a fragrant potpourri.

- Sprinkle the dried material with a few drops of oil in a chosen fragrance.

- Mix everything together to spread the oil around.

- Store the mixture in a lidded jar to cure.

- After a week, spoon some into a dish, refreshing the mixture with a few drops of oil, as necessary.

Collectibles

There is no limit to the kinds of collectibles that you can use to add emotional dimension to your bathroom decorating scheme. What is important is that the treasures hold personal meaning to you. Although it is necessary to consider the effects of humidity (a collection of embroidered silk purses might get ruined, for example), it should not deter you.

Line up pretty **perfume bottles** on **mirrored trays**, display **jars** of lotions and creams, or bubble bath and bath salts. Ornate **candlesticks** with interesting silhouettes can be placed on the ledge around the tub or the window sill. A collection of china boxes can be shown off on a polished counter. Large **vases** can be filled to overflowing with fresh flowers. Small vases can hold one bloom each.

Don't forget the walls: They are effective backdrops for collections of **china plates** and **painted tiles**. Small, framed **mirrors** can create geometric impact when they are placed in an organized grid; their surfaces will create a mosaic of reflections.

You can use restraint in displaying your collections, or you can be exuberant, paving the wall with every memento you have ever fallen in love with, as shown in the bathroom featured on the opposite page.

OPPOSITE

Illustrating the impact that collectibles can have in a bathroom is this eclectic mix of personal mementos, artifacts, and crafts used to decorate an entire wall in this bathroom. The arrangement is ordered and symmetrical, with a tall mirror forming the center of this well-defined collection. The reflection in the mirror shows a view of a shower curtain, the only visual cue that a traditional bathroom has been entered. The wall contains dried natural materials—roses, a lavender bouquet, and starfish. A lustrous tray made of hammered brass, a wooden cross, and a ceramic wall shelf cast in the shape of a cherub share the wall with a nonchalantly placed tassel in red. When an item has no identical twin, a substitute with the same contour and dimension can be used in its place. Filled with a seemingly lifelong accumulation of souvenir and talisman, the wall has been transformed into a kind of personal altar.

SOURCES AND RESOURCES

BOOKS

Ashwell, Rachel, and Glynis Costin. *Shabby Chic.* New York: Harper Collins, 1996.

Ashwell, Rachel, and Wynn Miller. *Shabby Chic: Treasure Hunting and Decorating Guide.* New York: Regan Books, 1998.

Cohen, Sacha. *The Practical Encyclopedia of Paint Recipes and Paint Effects: The Ultimate Source Book for Creating Beautiful, Easy-to-Achieve Interiors.* New York: Lorenz Books, 1999.

de Dampierre, Florence. *The Best of Painted Furniture.* New York: Rizzoli, 1987.

Drucker, Mindy, and Pierre Finkelstein. *Recipes for Surfaces: Decorative Paint Finishes Made Simple.* New York: Fireside, 1990.

Finkelstein, Pierre. *The Art of Faux: The Complete Sourcebook of Decorative Painted Finishes.* New York: Watson-Guptill Publications, 1997.

Lowther, Richard, and Lynne Robinson. *Decorative Paint Recipes: A Step-by-Step Guide to Finishing Touches for Your Home.* San Francisco: Chronicle Books, 1997.

McCloud, Kevin. *Decorative Style: The Most Original and Comprehensive Sourcebook of Styles, Treatments, Techniques, and Materials.* New York: Simon and Schuster, 1990.

Miller, Judith, and Martin Miller. *Period Finishes and Effects: A Step-by-Step Guide to Decorating Techniques.* New York: Rizzoli, 1992.

Moss, Charlotte. *A Passion for Detail.* New York: Doubleday, 1991.

Moulin, Pierre, Pierre Le Vec, and Linda Dannenberg. *Pierre Deux's French Country.* New York: Clarkson N. Potter, 1984.

Praz, Mario. *An Illustrated History of Interior Decoration: From Pompeii to Art Nouveau.* New York: Thames and Hudson, 1964.

Strasser, Claudia. *The Paris Apartment: Romantic Décor on a Flea Market Budget.* New York: Harper Collins, 1997.

Travis, Debbie, and Barbara Dingle. *Debbie Travis' Decorating Solutions: More Than 65 Paint and Plaster Finishes for Every Room in Your Home.* New York: Clarkson N. Potter, 1999.

Travis, Debbie, and Barbara Dingle. *Debbie Travis' Painted House.* New York: Clarkson N. Potter, 1997.

Wagstaff, Liz. *Paint Recipes: A Step-by-Step Guide to Colors and Finishes for the Home.* San Francisco: Chronicle Books, 1996.

RETAIL SOURCES

ABC Carpet & Home
888 Broadway
New York, NY 10003 USA
(212) 473-3000
www.abchome.com
home furnishings, furniture, fabric

Beadworks, Inc.
149 Water St.
Norwalk, CT 06854 USA
(203) 852-9108
www.beadworks.com
beads

B&J Fabric
263 W. 40th St.
New York, NY 10018 USA
(212) 354-8150
fabric

Budge and Coward
67 Roman Rd.
EZ London, UK
(020) 8980-8837
glasswork, ceramics, printmaking, and painting; showcases works of graduates of the Royal College of Art

California Closets
1000 Fourth St.
Suite 800
San Rafael, CA 94901
(800) 2SIMPLIFY
www.calclosets.com

Craft King
12750 W. Capitol Dr.
Brookfield, WI 53005 USA
(800) 373-3434
www.craftking.com
general craft supplies

Crate & Barrel
(800) 323-5461
www.crateandbarrel.com
home furnishings

Delta Technical Coating, Inc.
2550 Pellissier Pl.
Whittier, CA 90601 USA
(800) 423-4135
www.deltacrafts.com
general craft supplies

Dick Blick Art Materials
P.O. Box 1267
Galesburg, IL 61402-1267 USA
USA: (800) 828-4548
International: (309) 343-6181
www.dickblick.com
general craft supplies

De Tonge
152, Ave. de Malakoff
(Porte Maillot)
75116 Paris, France
01-45-02-14-02
www.detonge.com
French furniture, accessories, linen, and lighting

Echo
1433 Lonsdale Ave, #121
North Vancouver, V7M2H9 BC
(604) 980-8011
(800) 663-6004
www.echochina.com
buys and sells discontinued china and silver

Gardener's Eden
(800) 822-9600
www.gardenerseden.com
outdoor and indoor decorations, lighting, and furniture

SOURCES AND RESOURCES
(CONTINUED)

The Glidden Company
925 Euclid Ave.
Cleveland, OH 44115 USA
(800) GLIDDEN
www.gliddenpaint.com
paint

Gruppo Feg
0362-869313
www.gruppafeg.it
*Modern Italian furniture and home
furnishings available through retail outlets*

Guerra Paint and Pigment
510 E. 13th St.
New York, NY 10009 USA
(212) 529-0628
paint

Home Design Centre
2375 Dundas St. W.
Mississauga, Ontario
Canada
*furniture, accessories, do-it-yourself supplies
including paint and wall coverings*

IKEA
Catalog: (800) 434-4532
www.IKEA.com
home furnishings

JRM Beads Ltd.
16 Redbridge Enterprise Centre
Thompson Close
Ilford, Essex IG1 1TY, UK
(020) 8553-3240
email: tah@beadworks.co.uk
beads

Krylon Paints
Cleveland, OH 44115 USA
(800) 4-KRYLON
www.krylon.com
*specialty spray paints, faux stained glass,
stone, metals, pearls, antiques, and
mirror kits*

La Maison
107/108 Shoreditch High St.
London EI6JN, UK
(020) 7729-9646
French country antiques (especially beds)

Laura Ashley, Ltd.
Customer Service
Freepost SY1225
P.O. Box 19
Newtown
Powys SY16 1DZ UK
(0870) 562-2116
www.lauraashley.com
(800) 463-8075
www.laura-ashleyusa.com
*home furnishings, furniture, floor coverings,
and fabric*

Léron
750 Madison Ave.
New York, NY 10021 USA
(800) 954-6369
(212) 753-6700
www.leron.com
*couture linens for bed, bath, dining,
and entertaining*

Martha By Mail
P.O. Box 60060
Tampa, Fl 33660-0060 USA
(800) 950-7130
www.MarthaStewart.com
home furnishings

May Silk
16202 Distribution Way
Cerritos, CA 90703 USA
(562) 926-1818
www.maysilk.com
silk flowers and foliage

Michaels
The Arts and Crafts Store
850 N. Lake Dr., Suite 500
Coppell, TX 75019 USA
(800) MICHAELS
(800) 642-4235
www.michaels.com
general craft supplies

M&J Trim
1008 Sixth Ave.
New York, NY 10018 USA
(800) 9MJTRIM
(212) 842-5050
www.mjtrim.com
buttons, beads, and trims

Mokuba
55 W. 39th St.
New York, NY 10018 USA
(212) 869-8900
www.mokubany.com
ribbon and trim

N'est
1337 Greene Ave.
Montreal, Canada
(514) 939-6378
*vintage collectibles in porcelain and glass,
trays, chandeliers, small furniture*

Ornamental Resources, Inc.
P.O. Box 3010
1427 Miner St.
Idaho Springs, CO 80452 USA
(800) 876-6762
www.ornabead.com
beads

Pany Silk
146 W. 28th St.
New York, NY 10001 USA
(212) 645-9526
silk flowers and foliage

Pearl Paint
1033 E. Oakland Park Blvd.
Fort Lauderdale, FL 33334 USA
USA Mail Order: (800) 221-6845
International Mail Order: (954) 564-5700
ext. 37
www.pearlpaint.com
general craft supplies

Plaid Enterprises, Inc.
Norcross, GA 30091-7600 USA
(800) 842-4197
www.plaidonline.com
general craft supplies

Pierre Deux
625 Madison Ave.
New York, NY 10022 USA
(212) 521-8012
Customer Service: (888) 743-7732
www.pierredeux.com
French country fabrics, furnishings and
antiques

Pottery Barn
Catalog: (800) 922-5507
www.potterybarn.com
home furnishings

Restoration Hardware
Catalog: (800) 762-1005
www.restorationhardware.com
home furnishings

Sanderson
233 King's Rd.
London SW3, UK
(01) 895-8-30000
www.sanderson-online.co.uk
English furniture and home furnishings

Smith & Hawken
(800) 776-3336
www.SmithandHawken.com
outdoor furnishings and garden supplies

Sunshine Discount Crafts
12335 62nd St. North
Dept. Web
Largo, FL 33773 USA
USA Orders: (800) 729-2878
International Orders: (727) 538-2878
www.sunshinecrafts.com
general craft supplies

Toho Shoji
990 6th Ave.
New York, NY 10018 USA
(212) 868-7466
www.toho-shoji.com
beads

WORKSHOPS

Faux Filled Dreams
Gulf Coast
308 Highway 90, Suite E
Waveland, MS 39576 USA
(228) 446-0995
classes

California
422 Larkfield Center #290
Santa Rosa, CA 95403 USA
(707) 332-6545
www.fauxfilleddreams.com
classes

Faux Like A Pro
119 Braintree St.
Allston, MA 02134 USA
(617) 254-8898
www.fauxlikeapro.com
interactive classes, materials, and tools

Kelly S. King, Inc.
Institute of Decorative Finishes
A Division of the Faux Finish Institute™
13308 Millard Ave., Suite A
Omaha, NE 68137
(888) 560-FAUX
www.in-faux.com
classes

Mirage Studios
35-18 37th St.
Long Island City, NY 11103 USA
(718) 361-1071
www.miragefinishes.com
classes

Pro Faux
1367 Girard St.
Akron, OH 44301 USA
(800) PRO-FAUX
www.profaux.com
classes, materials and tools

The Faux Finish School
A Division of Martin Alan Hirsch
Decorative Finishes Studio
Louisville, KY
(800) 598-FAUX
www.fauxfinish.com
classes

The Pierre Finkelstein Institute of
Decorative Painting, Inc.
20 W. 20th St., Suite 1009
New York, NY 10011
(888) FAUX-ART
www.pfinkelstein.com
classes and materials

FLEA MARKETS

Bologna, Italy
Bologna Arte Antiquaria
Expo Information: 051-6487550
http://urp.comune.bologna.it

Brimfield, Mass.
Brimfield Antiques and Collectibles
www.brimfieldshow.com

New York, N.Y.
Chelsea Flea Market
23rd St., 6th–7th Ave.
weekends—old furniture, collectibles,
bric-a-brac

Paris, France
Porte de Cligancourt
Porte de Montreuil
huge markets with stalls and buildings filled
with old furniture, decorative accessories,
collectibles, and lighting

CREDITS

PHOTOGRAPHY CREDITS

Courtesy of Laura Ashley Ltd., 25; 32; 40; 62; 63; 66; 96; 102; 127; 134; 135

Courtesy of California Closets, 138

Steve Dalton/Red Cover, 110 (bottom)

Guillaume de Laubier, 2; 6 (left); 7 (right); 8; 20; 21; 23; 28; 38; 45; 49; 51; 52 (top); 55; 57; 59; 73; 75; 79; 81; 82; 86; 89; 95; 98; 108; 111; 113; 117; 119; 120; 122; 131

Richard Felber, 22; 24; 132

Courtesy of The Glidden Company, 78

Steve Gross & Susan Daley, 52 (bottom); 69

Steve Gross & Susan Daley/Gwen Griffith, Design, 42

Steve Gross & Susan Daley/Rebecca Purcell, Design, 109

Steve Gross & Susan Daley/Gayle Spannaus, Design, 13; 105

Mick Hales, 83; 107

Mick Hales/Anne LeConey, Design, 112

Brian Harrison/Red Cover, 16; 27; 93

Steven Mays/Elena Agostinis, Painter, 31; 46

Steven Mays/Richard C. Smith, Design, 54

Rob Melnychuk, 7 (middle); 87; 90; 101; 103; 137

Eric Roth, 7 (left); 19; 35; 37; 39; 41; 47; 60; 76; 84; 97; 106; 114; 125

Courtesy of Shabby Chic, 6 (right); 64

Tim Street-Porter, 129

Andreas von Einsiedel/Red Cover, 71; 74

DESIGN CREDITS

Gwen Griffith, San Antonio, Tex., p. 42
Rebecca Purcell, New York, N.Y., p. 109
Richard C. Smith, p. 54
Gayle Spannaus, New York, N.Y., pp. 13, 105

DECORATIVE PAINTING CREDIT

Elena Agostinis, pp. 31, 46

ABOUT THE AUTHORS

Carol Endler Sterbenz

Carol Endler Sterbenz is an editor and writer specializing in decorating and crafts. She has written more than twenty-five lifestyle and home decorating books and is a frequent guest on national television shows. She often travels to France where she is completing a large-scale work on French-style decorating. Ms. Sterbenz lives with her husband in New York City.

Genevieve A. Sterbenz

Genevieve A. Sterbenz is the author of six home decorating and craft books. She is a longtime contributing designer to lifestyle books and national magazines, and can frequently be seen on television presenting decorating ideas. She lives in New York City.

This is the fourth work of this mother-daughter team.